REASONS
For Hope

GateWay Publishing
5883 Eden Park Place
San Jose, California 95138

ISBN - 978-1985265493

Printed in the USA

For more information about GateWay City Church, visit

MyGateWayCity.Church

Table of Contents

Introduction

Pastor David Cannistraci

Our culture is in a crisis of conflicting beliefs. We have different political beliefs, religious viewpoints, cultural practices, and personal convictions. The complexity of life leaves many wondering if anything can be trusted or true. Can people in power be trusted? Can governments, politicians, banks, police, and educators all be trustworthy? How about organized religion? As a result, many people are confused and skeptical—trusting no one, believing in nothing.

Sometimes our beliefs let us down because they are not based in truth. Many of us grew up believing in God, but we also believed in Santa Claus, the Easter Bunny, and the Tooth Fairy. We are left to wonder…

Who can we really trust and what is really true?

In this, we long for clear and credible answers to our biggest spiritual questions:

> *Is it rational for you and I to believe in a literal Jesus who rose from the dead? Can we trust the Bible as a source of truth? Is there really a heaven, or is it just a myth? And what about God—does He exist? How can we know that, and if He is real, can He be trusted?*

The good news is that you don't have to throw your brains in the garbage can in order to be a person of faith. Life's most important questions can be answered reasonably and reliably. There are reasons for us to trust and reasons for us to believe. Most importantly…

There are reasons for us to hope!

That's what this series is all about. Life is about to get much more certain and sensible for you. Join us in this six-week study, and get ready to experience fresh hope in your life!

"But in your hearts revere Christ as Lord. Always be prepared to give an answer to everyone who asks you to give the REASON FOR THE HOPE that you have." 1 Peter 3:15

Pastor David

P.S. - This series is based in large part upon the excellent writings of my friend, Pastor Chip Ingram. I gratefully acknowledge his amazing contribution to our city, and to much of this study, and I joyfully recommend that everyone read his book WHY I BELIEVE (Baker Books, 2017).

What is included in this study?

Welcome to the REASONS for HOPE small group study guide. We are very excited about what God is going to do in and through you over the next six weeks. Each lesson has been prayerfully written and laid out for maximum impact in your life so that you can be that house which is built on a rock (Matthew 7:24ff).

There are three sections in this workbook to help you know and grow in the "REASONS for HOPE". They are as follows:

1. **Weekly Bible study**
   There are six weekly Bible studies that coincide with GateWay's Sunday morning services. The videos of the Sunday series will be posted to YouTube and on our website for your viewing.

2. **Further study and review**
   At the end of each study you will find a section on further study for those who desire additional notes, references, and the opportunity to "go a little deeper".

3. **Weekly devotional**
   One of the quickest ways to grow strong is to read, pray, and journal what God is doing in your life. We have included 42 devotionals, each based on the previous week's lesson. We encourage you to attend a small group, work through the Bible study, and then take time to hold your own personal devotions by reading, praying, and journaling.

Our prayer is that God's word and power come alive in you and all that you do as you go through this study. Get ready to be blessed!

Week One
Why We Believe in the Resurrection

VIDEO NOTES

_____

_____

_____

_____

_____

_____

WARM UP

1. Why is it that most of the news reports on T.V. and radio focus on the negative aspects of our culture?

2. When was the last time you heard really good news, either personally or about our nation? What was it?

3. Why is it that the resurrection of Jesus Christ is the greatest news in the history of mankind?

WORD

"If Christ has not been raised, then your faith is useless and you are still guilty of your sins. In that case, all who have died believing in Christ are lost! And...we are more to be pitied than anyone in the world." (1 Corinthians 15:17-19 NLT)

Week One Big Idea:

Christ's resurrection is foundational to the Christian faith and paves the way for a life of hope. It's where we must all begin. Either Jesus rose from the dead, or He's just another fanatical religious figure who should never be trusted. If He did actually rise from the dead, and if He is alive right now, then that's a much different story. The resurrection of Jesus from the dead becomes our first reason for hope.

Does it matter whether Jesus rose from the dead? Everything we believe about forgiveness of sins, the meaning of life, and the reality of heaven would be meaningless if Jesus is dead.

Let's discuss three reasons why we believe in the resurrection of Jesus Christ.

Reason #1 - Jesus was unlike anyone who has ever lived.

We believe in the resurrection because of the character of Jesus Christ. He lived a one-of-a-kind life and the resurrection was a one-of-a-kind event. There is no individual, no other religious or political leader, who can match the character, teaching intellect, and personal beauty of the Lord Jesus Christ.

"Who among you can prove me guilty of any sin? If I am telling you the truth, why don't you believe me?" (John 8:46 NET)

Throughout modern history, people have universally accepted the greatness of Jesus. Islam, Buddhism, and Hinduism all hold Christ in high regard, recognizing His character, love, and integrity. If He was truly great—and that cannot be disputed—then He can truly be trusted.

What are some of the reasons Jesus is unique and unprecedented throughout history?

_____

_____

_____

Reason #2 - Even Christ's enemies never challenged the reality of His miracles.

We believe in the resurrection because His works have never been invalidated. Jesus turned water into wine, fed multitudes, healed the sick, and raised the dead. One firsthand witness of Christ's miracles reported,

> _"Jesus also did many other things. If they were all written down, I suppose the whole world could not contain the books that would be written." (John 21:25 NLT)_

In all of these events, even the religious establishment who feared and hated him never once said, "You faked that miracle. That didn't really happen." The miracles kept coming and the crowds kept growing.

In that day, you could talk to the blind man who received his sight. You could interview the bride who drank new wine and the man who was instantly freed from the torment of 2,000 demons.

Today we have so many filters, animation tools, and special effects techniques to help us bend reality and make people believe things. But Jesus never used those tools. He didn't need them. His miracles were real, and that's another reason we believe in His miraculous resurrection.

Have you heard of, seen, or experienced a miracle or healing done today by Jesus Christ? What was it and how did it affect your life?

_____

_____

_____

Reason #3 - Jesus' identity as God's Son was confirmed again and again.

When someone's identity needs to be confirmed, investigators can arrange a series of interviews with a subject's friends or neighbors to confirm what is true or false. We can do something similar with regard to Christ's identity: we can confirm who He is by the testimony of those who are most credible.

We believe in the resurrection because the identity of Jesus was repeatedly confirmed. Consider the following three witnesses:

1. The fulfillment of Old Testament prophecy confirms His identity:

The Old Testament is filled with specific prophecies about Jesus made long before His birth. Isaiah predicted that Jesus would be born of a virgin (Isaiah 7:14), perform miracles (Isaiah 35:5-6), and be suffer and called the Lord (Isaiah 7:14). The prophet Micah predicted his birth in Bethlehem (Micah 5:2), and the book of Psalms predicted He would descend from David (Psalm 110:1), be crucified, rise from the dead, and ascend to heaven (Psalm 22).

There are over 700 of these prophecies, all of which Jesus fulfilled. If each of these came true, it is further testament to the credibility of Christ, including His resurrection.

2. **God the Father affirmed Christ's unique identity:**

"John baptized Jesus in the Jordan River. As Jesus was coming up out of the water…A voice came from heaven and said, 'You are my Son, the one I love. I am very pleased with you.'" (Mark 1:9-11 ERV)

3. **Finally, Jesus Himself claimed to be God:**

"Jesus said to him, 'I am the way, the truth, and the life. No one comes to the Father except through Me.'" (John 14:6 NKJV)

There are many other credible witnesses that could be called concerning the identity of Christ. The point is, with so much evidence, it's hard to doubt that Jesus is who He said He is and that He rose from the dead.

Are you convinced Jesus Christ rose from the dead? Why?
Review the above three reasons and share which one gives you the full confidence to know and trust the risen Savior.

Conclusion

What have we learned? Jesus was a unique and universally respected person. His life and character cannot be questioned. His enemies and detractors could not defeat Him. His miracles were undeniable. He was the Son of God and the case for His resurrection is more than believable.

APPLICATION

1. Discuss why the reality of the resurrection of Jesus Christ has such a powerful impact on your life.

2. What changes in your life have taken place since receiving the risen Lord?

3. Can you now confidently share the resurrection story with your unsaved friends and family?

PRAYER

1. Pray for anyone who has a need in their life and believe God for a miracle to take place.

2. Pray for a new and fresh commitment to Jesus Christ as Lord and Savior knowing He is raised from the dead.

3. Pray for each member of the group to have the opportunity to share the resurrection story with someone else they know this week and invite that person to the group.

Digging Deeper

Did Jesus really rise from the dead? Please explain[1].

Most would agree about the essential events surrounding Jesus' death. He was crucified, buried, Roman guards made the tomb secure, the grave was sealed, and three days later the tomb was empty. Historical evidence strongly supports these events. But some even today believe there was some other explanation for the empty tomb.

Let's discuss three theories some critics adhere too.

1. The Swoon Theory (also called the Resuscitation Theory)

The Swoon Theory, first proposed in 1828 by H. E. G. Paulus, a German theologian and critic of the Bible, claims that Jesus did not die. Rather, suggested Paulus, Jesus merely *fainted* on the cross, from pain, shock, and loss of blood. Jesus was then mistakenly buried alive.

The **Swoon Theory** suggests that the cool, damp air of the tomb somehow revived Jesus after three days, and He decided to exit. Despite not having access to needed medical care and nourishment, Jesus supposedly managed to unwrap His dressings and then, in the total darkness of the tomb, locate and roll away the mammoth stone sealing the tomb entrance. And then, *still unnoticed by the guards*, Jesus supposedly walked away, on feet punctured by the nails of the cross, to rejoin His disciples.

In his article, **A Lawyer Examines The Swoon Theory**, Texas attorney Joseph "Rick" Reinckens satirically unpacks this theory. I will just share a snippet of this must-read:

---

[1] **Josh McDowell Ministry** - https://www.josh.org/resurrection-theories-debunked

"Even in His weakened condition, in a quiet private cemetery, Jesus manages to push back the stone door without any of the guards noticing! Why go half-way? Jesus has been whipped, beaten and stabbed, is hemorrhaging, and hasn't had any food or drink for at least three days. Does He just push the stone open enough to squeeze through? No, He pushes the stone door COMPLETELY out of the way!!!"

Could the Roman soldiers have been asleep? Is that how Jesus supposedly made His sneaky escape?

Peter Kreeft, a popular writer of Christian philosophy, theology, and apologetics, says there is no way:

"The story the Jewish authorities spread, that the guards fell asleep and the disciples stole the body, is unbelievable. Roman guards would not fall asleep on a job like that; if they did, they would lose their lives. And even if they did fall asleep, the crowd and the effort and the noise it would have taken to move an enormous boulder would have wakened them."

This resurrection theory is ludicrous. We can cross it off the list of possibility.

2. The Hallucination Theory

The **Hallucination Theory** asserts that the many people who saw Jesus in His resurrected body just *imagined* doing so. It's important to note that hallucinations come from *within a person*, not outside a person. Meaning hallucinations are entirely subjective. Science tells us that, generally, only particular kinds of people have hallucinations: persons who are paranoid or schizophrenic, or people under the influence of drugs.

The New Testament tells us, however, that all kinds of people saw Jesus after His resurrection, all of different ages, different occupations, different backgrounds, different viewpoints.

Adds Dr. Michael Licona, a professor of theology:

"Hallucinations are like dreams. They are private occurrences ... You could not share a hallucination you were having with someone any more than you could wake up your spouse in the middle of the night and ask him or her to join you in a dream you were having."

Hallucinations do not cause people to change or create new beliefs. The fact that many people chose to believe in Jesus, after talking with Him and touching His wounds, also helps to refute this theory. Hallucinations are an individual event. If 500 people have the same hallucination, that's a bigger miracle than the resurrection.

Cross this resurrection theory off the list of possibilities.

3. The Conspiracy Theory

The fact that the Bible tells us that lots of people saw Jesus over a 40-day period helps us to debunk this final theory. The Conspiracy Theory suggests that Christ's disciples simply stole His body and fabricated the resurrection story.

The great historian Eusebius (A.D. 314-318) was the first to argue that it is inconceivable that such a well-planned and thought-out conspiracy could succeed. Eusebius satirically imagined how the disciples might have motivated each other to take this route:

Let us band together to invent all the miracles and resurrection appearances which we never saw and let us carry the sham even to death!

Why not die for nothing? Why dislike torture and whipping inflicted for no good reason? Let us go out to all the nations and overthrow their institutions and denounce their gods! And even if we don't convince anybody, at least we'll have the satisfaction of drawing down on ourselves the punishment for our own deceit.

Adds Paul E. Little, author of *Know What You Believe*:

"Men will die for what they believe to be true, though it may actually be false. They do not, however, die for what they know is a lie."

Cross this resurrection theory off the list of possibility as well.

Conclusion

Isn't it interesting that people are able to believe a theory full of holes, but are unable to believe the truth? Jesus' disciples—though they faced horrendous persecution and all but one was martyred—never renounced their belief in the resurrection of Jesus! I'll go out on a limb here and say it's because they knew the resurrection to be true.

Why is it that so many people would rather believe a lie or fallacy and not the truth of the resurrection of Jesus Christ?

_____

_____

_____

_____

_____

Daily Devotionals

One of the best ways to stay strong and grow in your Christian walk is to take the time to read and journal through a daily devotional. Knowing this, we have included in this study guide 42 daily devotionals that coincide with the topical study for each week.

Structure of the devotionals

Each devotional includes four elements that will help you learn and apply these concepts to your lives.

1. **Scripture**
   It goes without saying that God's word is the source and basis of our Christian walk and is also the basis from which we start each day.

2. **Observation**
   After you read and meditate on the scripture, write down how the verse applies to your life.

3. **Application**
   Next, write down how you will apply the truth to your life.

4. **Prayer**
   Close the day by writing out a short prayer to the Lord, offering thanks, praise, repentance, or even a prophetic declaration.

Stay consistent in your devotionals and you will find over time that you get stronger and live a fruitful, overcoming life in Jesus!

Daily Devotional– Day 1

"Jesus said to her, 'I am the resurrection and the life. He who believes in Me, though he may die, he shall live. And whoever lives and believes in Me shall never die. Do you believe this?'" (John 11:25-26 NKJV)

The resurrection of Jesus Christ is more than an event in history. It is a person. Jesus Christ is the resurrection. What this means is that as God He is life, eternal life, and that life or power flows in Him and through Him to you. You see, when you receive Christ, He comes and dwells in you. And when He lives in you, His resurrection power lives in you too. You, today, have resurrection life residing in you because of the life that is in Jesus.

It is His life in you that imparts the life of Heaven, the power to overcome sin and defeat, and the power to live forever with Him. So today, thank God for the resurrection life that is in Christ and now lives in you. Thank God for Jesus rising from dead. Thank God that the resurrection now causes you to live forever too . . . with Him!

This is what today's verse means to me.

_____

_____

_____

_____

_____

Here is how I can apply this truth in my life.

_____

_____

_____

_____

_____

_____

This is my prayer for today.

_____

_____

_____

_____

_____

_____

_____

Daily Devotional– Day 2

"Blessed be the God and Father of our Lord Jesus Christ, who according to His abundant mercy has begotten us again to a living hope through the resurrection of Jesus Christ from the dead." (1 Peter 1:3 NKJV)

Many around us who don't know Christ, lives are lives without hope. Their trust is in a variety of other things which are only temporary. People hope to get a better job, more money, or that perfect relationship. When things don't work out, their lives fall apart. This is why there is so much depression and anxiety around us. People try to fill that void in their soul with things or people who let them down.

But the hope we have in Christ raises us up above life's circumstances and gives us a reason to live. Material things come and go, but knowing that you're saved and will live forever will sustain you in even in the darkness of days. So today, thank God for Jesus giving you a hope that never changes, never fades away, and will always be with you, empowering you day by day. Thank God for the joy of His hope that can never be taken away. – AMEN!

This is what today's verse means to me.

_____

_____

_____

_____

_____

Here is how I can apply this truth in my life.

_____

_____

_____

_____

_____

_____

This is my prayer for today.

_____

_____

_____

_____

_____

_____

_____

_____

Daily Devotional– Day 3

"But God, who is rich in mercy, because of His great love with which He loved us, ⁵ even when we were dead in trespasses, made us alive together with Christ (by grace you have been saved), ⁶ and raised us up together, and made us sit together in the heavenly places in Christ Jesus." (Ephesians 2:4-5 NKJV)

Notice the words, "made us alive together" and "made us sit together". What does this mean? It means, the moment you were born again something supernatural occurred which connected you with Jesus Christ, and you were made alive just as He was made alive at the resurrection. And just as He was raised up, so you too were raised up and seated with Christ together with Him.

Today, you live with Christ having been raised with Him. Where is Christ? He's at the right hand of the Father. So, where are you? Also at the right hand of the Father. You're actually living in two locations at once. One is your earthly home; but since you were also raised up with Christ, you are seated with Him and have a heavenly residence, far above all principalities and powers. Praise God that you are raised up with Christ. Thank God for living with Him, close to Him, and being alive because of Him.

This is what today's verse means to me.

_____

_____

_____

Here is how I can apply this truth in my life.

_____

_____

_____

_____

_____

_____

This is my prayer for today.

_____

_____

_____

_____

_____

_____

_____

_____

Daily Devotional– Day 4

"I want to know Christ—yes, to know the power of his resurrection and participation in his sufferings, becoming like him in his death." (Philippians 3:10 NLT)

Did the Apostle Paul know Christ? Yes. But there was something else He wanted to know that gripped his heart, and that thing was the power of His resurrection. Paul wanted to identify with Jesus Christ: His death, suffering, and ultimately the power of His resurrection. You see, it was the power of the resurrection that flowed in Paul's veins and sustained him. It was through knowing Christ's suffering and resurrection that Paul could face each and every challenge and overcome, just as Jesus overcame.

What this means to you is regardless of what life situation comes your way, you have the power to overcome. Draw close to Christ and tell Him you want to know the power of His resurrection, the power to live, and the grace to rise above life's challenges like Him, you can overcome all things!

This is what today's verse means to me.

_____

_____

_____

_____

_____

Here is how I can apply this truth in my life.

_____

_____

_____

_____

_____

_____

This is my prayer for today.

_____

_____

_____

_____

_____

_____

_____

Daily Devotional– Day 5

"Now it came to pass, when the time had come for Him to be received up, that He steadfastly set His face to go to Jerusalem." (Luke 9:51 NKJV)

"For the Lord GOD will help Me; therefore, I will not be disgraced; therefore, I have set My face like a flint, and I know that I will not be ashamed." (Isaiah 50:7 NKJV)

Notice the words, *"set his face"*. This phrase is taken from the book of Isaiah the prophet where we read, *"I have set my face like a flint"*. Jesus knew His assignment was to die on a cross for mankind's sins, bear the weight of their guilt and shame, and then rise again. And He faced this extremely difficult challenge with boldness and audacious confidence. He did not tip-toe into Jerusalem with fear and doubt. Instead He set his face and took the challenge head-on, knowing He was going to overcome.

How often do we face our challenges with fear, uncertainty, doubt, and apprehension? How often do we allow circumstances to win over us instead of us winning over them? "Set your face" and overcome challenge life throws your way. Thank God for the victory in everything you do. Now go face the storms!

This is what today's verse means to me.

_____

_____

_____

Here is how I can apply this truth in my life.

_____

_____

_____

_____

_____

_____

This is my prayer for today.

_____

_____

_____

_____

_____

_____

_____

Daily Devotional– Day 6

"Now may the God of peace who brought up our Lord Jesus from the dead, that great Shepherd of the sheep, through the blood of the everlasting covenant, ²¹ make you complete in every good work to do His will, working in you⁽ᶻ⁾ what is well pleasing in His sight, through Jesus Christ, to whom be glory forever and ever. Amen." (Hebrews 13:20-21 NKJV)

Wow! There is a lot in this verse that can have a major impact on your life. Jesus was brought up from the dead through the blood of the covenant. This shows the power of His blood that He gave on the cross. It was the blood of Jesus that broke the power of sin and death.

Now notice it is "the God of peace" who works in you to "make you complete" and do His will. What this verse means is that the blood of the covenant sealed the deal and forever stands as the basis for your new life and the continuing power of God to change you, mold you, and equip you to live as a conqueror in this world. He is working in you, living in you, empowering you to overcome through the power of the blood of Jesus and the life of the resurrection.

Today, thank God He is working in your life. He is actively strengthening you, leading you, and working in what is pleasing in His sight.

This is what today's verse means to me.

_____

_____

_____

_____

_____

Here is how I can apply this truth in my life.

_____

_____

_____

_____

_____

_____

This is my prayer for today.

_____

_____

_____

_____

_____

Daily Devotional– Day 7

"Therefore, we were buried with Him through baptism into death, that just as Christ was raised from the dead by the glory of the Father, even so we also should walk in newness of life." (Romans 6:4 NKJV)

We should walk in newness of life. This is the life God intended us to live. A life filled with Jesus' peace, joy, and blessing; a life overcoming sin and entering into the fullness of Christ's life. This newness of life is a life of triumph and victory. This is a life filled with confidence, boldness, and assurance that all things work for good.

The reason this verse is so vital to our understanding is that for many Christians, their life is no different than before they were born again. Yes, they have eternal life off into the future. But what about life now? What about living above sin and fear now, today? Is it possible to live a life that always leads us into triumph (2 Cor. 2:14)?

Today, you can choose to live in newness of life. You can live this new life today, right here, right now. God has made His life available to you and wants to make it real through you. So today, thank God for the life of Christ living in you. Boldly confess that you walk in newness of life. Believe it, walk in it, and His life will come alive in you!

This is what today's verse means to me.

_____

_____

_____

_____

Here is how I can apply this truth in my life.

_____

_____

_____

_____

_____

_____

This is my prayer for today.

_____

_____

_____

_____

_____

_____

_____

_____

What did God do in my life this week?

What did Jesus Christ do in and through you this past week? What did the Holy say to you? What prayers were answered? Who did you share Christ with? What good thing can you thank God for? Write out the difference this week made in your life.

_____

_____

_____

_____

_____

_____

_____

_____

_____

_____

_____

_____

_____

_____

Week Two
Did Jesus Really Die?

VIDEO NOTES

_____

_____

_____

_____

_____

_____

WARM UP

1. Why is death and dying so hard for people who don't know Jesus Christ?

2. Do you think there will be animals in Heaven? What happens to our pets when they die? Do they go to Heaven?

3. What do you think the Roman guards thought when they saw Jesus walking out of the tomb on resurrection day?

"Jesus said to her, 'I am the resurrection and the life. He who believes in Me, though he may die, he shall live. And whoever lives and believes in Me shall never die. Do you believe this?'" (John 11:25-26 NKJV)

Week Two Big Idea:

Our culture is fascinated with the idea of coming back from the dead. There are countless movies and television shows on the topic. From vampires to zombies to ghostly afterlife experiences, many spend time and money imagining a return from death. But has anyone ever done it? And if so, why would that be important to us?

This promise of Jesus concerning eternal life would be laughable apart from the resurrection. Some believe Jesus Christ was merely a great teacher, but a great teacher would never make such a claim. He is either God's Son or the craziest lunatic in history. Each of us must consider the evidence and determine for ourselves if He provides us with reasons for hope.

Last week we discovered three reasons for the resurrection. Let's continue our journey together and cover some more reasons why we can believe in the resurrection and live a life of hope.

Reason #4 - The death of Jesus was indisputable.

We believe in the resurrection of Jesus because the evidence is clear that he actually died. Some have advanced the idea that Jesus was merely unconscious and not dead. This "swoon theory" is an attempt to disprove Christianity. If Jesus never died He could not have risen from the dead.

Jesus did die, and the following reasons leave little room for doubt:

1. **Pilate and the centurions said He was dead.**

"Pilate was surprised that he was already dead. He called the centurion and asked him if he had been dead for some time. When Pilate was informed by the centurion, he gave the body to Joseph." (Mark 15:44-45 NET)

Though it was customary in crucifixion for the victims' legs to be broken to insure a quicker death, the Roman soldiers did not break Jesus's legs because he had already died (John 19:33,36). Later they even pierced his side to further confirm his death.

2. Medical science says He could not have survived.

The movie *The Passion of the Christ* is a brutal but accurate portrayal of the process of whipping and beating which Christ endured. It was designed to bruise and tear the flesh off of one's bones. A crown of thorns was forced onto his head, and He was then taken to be violently crucified.

To confirm his death, a Roman soldier pierced Christ's side with a spear, bringing a sudden flow of blood and water (John 19:34). Medically, when this happens, death has most certainly occurred. The intensity of this ordeal from a medical perspective leaves little doubt that Jesus died.

3. Those who buried him knew he was dead.

Joseph of Arimathea along with a team of loving disciples took the body of Jesus and buried it in a tomb (John 19:38-40). They prepared Jesus's body according to burial practices at that time. Using up to 70 pounds of linen and ointments, His entire body was wrapped, including his face, mouth and nose. There is simply no way Christ could have survived this even if the cross had not already killed Him.

Who can we trust—those who say Christ did not die or those who say he died and rose from the dead? We believe the truth is obvious.

With the evidence of Jesus' death so strong, why is it that many people still refuse to accept the fact that He did die?

_____

_____

_____

Reason #5 - The burial of Jesus was public and secure.

"Pilate said to them, 'You have a guard; go your way, make it as secure as you know how.' [66] *So they went and made the tomb secure, sealing the stone and setting the guard." (Matthew 27:65ff)*

Some skeptics admit that Jesus must have died, but then assert that the disciples stole his body (meaning that He did not rise from the dead). We believe in the resurrection because there is no way that this could have happened.

Because the Pharisees were concerned that the resurrection would take place, they begged Pilate for help (Matthew 27:62-66). Pilate responded by placing Roman guards to watch the tomb, making it as secure as possible. The chief priests then decided to bribe the soldiers to say that the disciples stole Christ's body while they slept (Matthew 28:11-13). They reasoned that sleeping guards could not witness Christ's body being stolen.

The problem is that the Roman army (the largest, best-organized fighting force in the world) meted out capital punishment for anyone who failed at their duties. No Roman soldier would ever have conspired with a Jew to lie or to allow a body they were guarding to be stolen. Besides, no one was ever able to produce a body. It's hard to argue that someone is dead when you have no body! The clear truth is Jesus is not dead, but alive.

Why couldn't the Jewish authorities allow the guards to tell the truth about Jesus' resurrection? Why did they have to bribe them?

Reason #6 - ALL the evidence is overwhelming.

In a court of law, to win a case you must present evidence that is convincing beyond a reasonable doubt. We believe in the resurrection because of the mountain of evidence. Books have been written to present the legal evidence; we offer here in this brief lesson just a few important points.

1. **Jesus predicted His death and resurrection.**

   "From that time Jesus began to show his disciples that he must go to Jerusalem and suffer many things from the elders and chief priests and scribes, and be killed, and on the third day be raised." (Matthew 16:21 ESV)

2. **The resurrected Jesus appeared 12 times to over 500 witnesses.**

   "He was seen by Peter and then by the Twelve. After that, he was seen by more than 500 of his followers at one time, most of whom

are still alive...Then he was seen by James and later by all the apostles." (1 Corinthians 15:5-7 NLT)

"For forty days after his death he appeared to them many times in ways that proved beyond doubt that he was alive. They saw him, and he talked with them about the Kingdom of God." (Acts 1:3 GNT)

Imagine over 500 people swearing that they'd personally seen Christ alive. Men, women, believers, doubters, people whom Jesus had spoken with, ate with, and even invited to touch His wounds. Not one person has been able to disprove the clear evidence of the resurrection.

Even with the many appearances of Jesus Christ after the resurrection, why is it that many still did not believe?

_____

_____

_____

3. The doubting disciples were utterly transformed.

Changed lives are the ultimate proof of the resurrection. Before Easter, the disciples were dejected, believing Jesus was gone forever. Peter had denied Him. They'd fled and hidden, grieving and afraid. But after the resurrection, these same men were transformed. They believed He was alive because they'd seen Him and spoken to Him. Within days, they were boldly proclaiming Jesus is alive. They went from selfish and dejected men to powerful spiritual leaders who transformed the world with their message about Christ, most of them dying as martyrs for their testimony.

What do you think gave the disciples such boldness to preach and give their lives for the gospel after the resurrection?

_____

_____

_____

How has your life changed since believing and knowing the power of the resurrection of Christ?

_____

_____

_____

Share an example of someone you have led to Christ and what the power of the resurrection meant in their life.

_____

_____

_____

_____

_____

Conclusion

For the last 2000 years, billions of lives have been radically changed by the Risen Christ. Kings have tried to stop them, philosophers hoped to disprove them, and civilizations have conspired to silence them. But the evidence of the resurrection and the message of the gospel have proven too great: Jesus Christ really did die, and He really did rise again!

APPLICATION

1. What is the strongest evidence to you that Jesus Christ did indeed rise from the dead?

2. Of the six reasons presented, which ones can you use to share with your family and friends to help them come to know Christ?

3. How does the proof of Jesus' resurrection help you overcome the challenges and battles of life today?

PRAYER

1. Pray for the members of the group to know, believe, and stand strong in the power of the resurrection in their lives.

2. Pray regarding any struggles and challenges anyone may be facing, and pray that the risen Savior again will show Himself alive in their lives.

3. Pray for each member of the group to have the opportunity to both share the resurrection story with someone else they know this week and invite them to the group.

Digging Deeper

What the Bible Says About Jesus' Tomb[2]

1. The tomb was a new one that had never been occupied.

   "Then he took it down, wrapped it in linen cloth and placed it in a tomb cut in the rock, one in which no one had yet been laid." (Luke 23:53)

2. No other bodies were there to be confused with that of Jesus.

3. It was hewn out of solid rock.

   "Joseph took the body, wrapped it in a clean linen cloth, and placed it in his own new tomb that he had cut out of the rock." (Matthew 27:59-60)

4. It was near the city of Jerusalem and accessible for investigation.

The Precautions at The Tomb: The Stone, The Roman Seal, And The Guard

The precautions taken at the tomb consisted of three things - the large stone, the Roman seal, and the guard.

1. The Stone
The Bible says that a large stone was rolled in front of the tomb of Jesus.

---

[2] Don Stewart – BlueLetterBible
https://www.blueletterbible.org/faq/don_stewart/don_stewart_247.cfm

"Joseph took the body, wrapped it in a clean linen cloth, and placed it in his own new tomb that he had cut out of the rock. He rolled a big stone in front of the entrance to the tomb and went away." (Matthew 27:59)

This stone would not only have sealed the tomb, but it also would have made it difficult for someone to come right in and steal the body.

2. The Roman Seal
The Roman seal was also placed over the tomb.

"And they went and made the grave secure, and along with the guard they set a seal on the stone." (Matthew 27:66)

The seal was sign of authentication that the tomb was occupied and the power and authority of Rome stood behind the seal. Anyone found breaking the Roman seal would suffer the punishment of an unpleasant death.

3. The Guard
A guard watched Jesus' tomb. This was either the Roman guard or the Jewish temple police.

"Pilate said to them, 'You have a guard; go, make it as secure as you know how.' And they went and made the grave secure, and along with the guard they set a seal on the stone." (Matthew 27:65-66)

There is a question as to which one of the two groups was watching over it. The context seems to favor the Roman guard. The Roman guard was a sixteen-man unit that was governed by very strict rules. Each member was responsible for six square feet of space. The guard members could not sit down or lean against anything while they were on duty. If a guard member fell asleep, he was beaten and burned with his own clothes. But he was not the only one executed; the entire sixteen-man guard unit was executed if only one of the members fell asleep while on duty.

The Religious Leaders Felt Secure
These precautions made the religious rulers feel secure that the excitement around Jesus would soon go away. Jesus lay dead in the tomb, and His frightened disciples had scattered and gone into hiding. They thought that they had won.

The Event That Changed the World

But the story was not over. The Bible says that early Sunday morning, certain women came to the tomb to anoint the body of Jesus. The stone had been removed, the seal had been broken, and the body was gone. An angel at the tomb asked:

> "Why do you seek the living among the dead? He is not here, but is risen." (Luke 24:5-6)

They went back to tell the other disciples, who at first did not believe their report.

> "And these words appeared to them as nonsense, and they would not believe them." (Luke 24:11)

However, they were persuaded to look for themselves, and they also found the tomb empty. This caused them confusion. The confusion vanished as the resurrected Christ first appeared to Mary Magdalene, then to some other women, and finally to the disciples. After being with the disciples for forty days, Jesus ascended into heaven. Ten days later, the disciples publicly proclaimed to all Jerusalem, and to the world, the fact that Jesus Christ had risen from the dead.

Where's the body?

Here we are, some 2000 years after the resurrection of Jesus Christ, and skeptics still have not provided a plausible explanation of where the body of Jesus ended up.

All the Jewish authorities and Roman government had to do to shut down this group of believers was to find the body. But they couldn't, so various theories and explanations have existed over to time to try to reconcile this historical event.

The bottom line is this. Every person must make a decision about the empty tomb. Fact: the tomb of Christ was empty and still is. Now it's incumbent upon those who deny it to explain what happened and wrestle with Christ's word and need of repentance, and receive His salvation.

Summary

Although the religious leaders felt satisfied when they handed Jesus over to Pontius Pilate to be crucified, they remembered Jesus' words that He would come back from the dead. Consequently, they asked Pilate to make the tomb as secure as possible. This consisted of a guard, either Roman or Jewish, a large stone rolled at the entrance of the tomb, and the Roman seal. However, these precautions were worthless when it came to stopping the tomb from being empty on Easter Sunday. The disciples were not able to steal the body - Jesus came back from the dead!

Notes:

Daily Devotional– Day 8

"If we have been united together in the likeness of His death, certainly we also shall be in the likeness of His resurrection, knowing this that our old man was crucified with Him, that the body of sin might be done away with, that we should no longer be slaves of sin." (Romans 6:5 NKJV)

Every believer needs to know that we are to identify with Christ's death in order for us to enter into the likeness of His resurrection. What this means is that just as Christ died and carried our sin, so our old man, old ways, and old habits need to die so that His life can now be experienced. We are to have our old man crucified so that sin may be done away with. How is this done? By receiving Jesus as Lord, our old inner man dies. But then each day it's a continual choice for us to live for Christ and turn away from sin. The good news is that the same power that gave Jesus victory over death is now available to us as well. We now today have the power to overcome sin so that we can be united together in His likeness of victory and power. Believe it – and live it!

This is what today's verse means to me.

_____

_____

_____

_____

_____

Here is how I can apply this truth in my life.

_____

_____

_____

_____

_____

This is my prayer for today.

_____

_____

_____

_____

_____

_____

Daily Devotional– Day 9

"The death he died, he died to sin once for all; but the life he lives, he lives to God. In the same way, count yourselves dead to sin but alive to God in Christ Jesus." (Romans 6:10-11 NKJV)

You don't have to wait until eternity to start living the power and victory of the resurrection. You can, today, become *"alive to God in Christ Jesus"*. It is as we turn from sin, dying to our old habits and ways, that the true power of the resurrection comes alive in us, and we can experience Christ's power today! But this is conditioned upon continually choosing to turn away from and consider ourselves dead to sin and alive to Christ. So today, make a choice to live free from and above sin. Stay in the place of close fellowship with the Holy Spirit. Thank God for His quickening power and anointing to be alive to Him today.

This is what today's verse means to me.

_____

_____

_____

_____

_____

_____

Here is how I can apply this truth in my life.

_____

_____

_____

_____

_____

_____

This is my prayer for today.

_____

_____

_____

_____

_____

_____

Daily Devotional– Day 10

"That I may know Him and the power of His resurrection, and the fellowship of His sufferings, being conformed to His death." (Phil. 3:10 NKJV)

In today's verse the Apostle Paul prays for four things. The first is to know Jesus. Next is the power of His resurrection. Thirdly is the fellowship of His sufferings, and lastly to be confirmed to His death. Why would Paul want to experience the fellowship of His sufferings and death? To know Christ's suffering and death is how Paul was able to continue through His hard times knowing that as he suffered, he was really tasting what it was like for Christ to suffer. But the good news is that as Christ suffered, overcame, and rose again, we know that when we go through hard times, we are really sensing what it was like for Christ. But we don't stop there. Because contained in every hardship, trial and challenge is the promise of resurrection, hope, and victory. Are you going through hard times? Know this, as Christ suffered and rose again, even so you too will rise again. Believe it!

This is what today's verse means to me.

_____

_____

_____

_____

_____

Here is how I can apply this truth in my life.

_____

_____

_____

_____

_____

_____

_____

This is my prayer for today.

_____

_____

_____

_____

_____

_____

_____

Daily Devotional– Day 11

"He died for all, that those who live should live no longer for themselves, but for Him who died for them and rose again." (2 Corinthians 5:15 NKJV)

Before a person comes to Christ their life pretty much centers on their interests, desires, and sometimes selfish ways. But when we come to Christ, the focus of our life is no longer ourselves but Him. Yes, Jesus is the one to whom and for whom we live. He is the centerpiece of all we do. He is our strength, our joy, our purpose, and our reason for life. It's when we *"no longer live for ourselves but for Him"*, that we experience all He has for us. As we live for Him, He lives through us.

Living for Christ opens up the door for all of Heaven's blessings. Living our lives for Him promises hope, purpose, grace, and abilities. When you start experiencing all that He has for us you'll never want to turn back to your older ways of living for yourself. Today, make a choice to continue living, loving, and serving Christ with all you have. Don't live for yourself today. Live for and in Him, and watch what He'll do for you!

This is what today's verse means to me.

_____

_____

_____

_____

_____

Here is how I can apply this truth in my life.

_____

_____

_____

_____

_____

_____

_____

This is my prayer for today.

_____

_____

_____

_____

_____

_____

_____

Daily Devotional– Day 12

"For the law of the Spirit of life in Christ Jesus has made me free from the law of sin and death." (Romans 8:2 NKJV)

The Spirit of life entered into the dead corpse of Jesus Christ and He came alive, was resurrected and even today now continues living as the Lord over all through the Spirit of life in and through Him. What's amazing is that the moment you were born again, the same Spirit of life, from Jesus, came into your dead soul and caused you to be born again. Further, that Spirit of life is available to you on a continual basis to deliver you and keep you free from the law of sin, death, doubt, fear, worry, sickness, poverty, and anything else that would rob you of victory.

So today, thank God for the Spirit in you. Confess out loud, "the law of the Spirit of life now lives in me and causes me to triumph in victory over all my enemies". Then from this day forward, thank God for His life and anointing to fill you fresh each day and stay strong in His spirit of life. – AMEN!

This is what today's verse means to me.

Here is how I can apply this truth in my life.

_____

_____

_____

_____

_____

_____

_____

This is my prayer for today.

_____

_____

_____

_____

_____

_____

_____

Daily Devotional– Day 13

"But if the Spirit of Him who raised Jesus from the dead dwells in you, He who raised Christ from the dead will also give life to your mortal bodies through His Spirit who dwells in you." (Romans 8:11 NKJV)

Read this powerful verse through several times and then meditate on its truth. Just think, the same Spirit that raised Christ from the dead lives in you. This alone is mind blowing. The dead body of Jesus lay on the stone, cold, wrapped in grave clothes and silent. Then all of a sudden on that Sunday morning the Holy Spirit and the glory of the Father entered every cell of His dead body and He came alive.

What this means for you is that the same Holy Spirit is available for you today. It's the same Spirit that can enter your body and heal you from sickness, deliver you from bondage, and cause you to overcome in all things. So be filled again today with the Spirit of Life. Allow the Holy Spirit to quicken, strengthen and heal you. You too can come alive and stay alive because of His Spirit living big inside you. AMEN!

This is what today's verse means to me.

_____

_____

_____

_____

_____

Here is how I can apply this truth in my life.

_____

_____

_____

_____

_____

_____

This is my prayer for today.

_____

_____

_____

_____

_____

_____

Daily Devotional– Day 14

"I have been crucified with Christ; it is no longer I who live, but Christ lives in me; and the life which I now live in the flesh I live by faith in the Son of God, who loved me and gave Himself for me." (Galatians 2:2 NKJV)

When you came to Christ, gave your life to Him, repented, and asked Him to be your Lord, you also entered into His death and crucifixion. The miracle of being born again is that your old man died and you now have become alive in Christ. You have been crucified with Christ. When Christ died, your sins were carried upon Him. Now it is not you and your old ways that live, but rather you live a new life, the life that comes from Jesus Christ.

But do you consider your old life and ways dead in Jesus? You need to recognize that your past failures, hurts, wounds, mistakes and guilt are now dead in Christ. This is a legal transaction. But you need to make it a reality by choosing today to *"live by faith in the Son of God"*. So today, thank God for dying to the old, and choosing to live alive to God. Let His life fill all that you are mentally, emotionally, and spiritually. In so doing, you'll have a new life, a blessed life – do it!

This is what today's verse means to me.

_____

_____

_____

_____

Here is how I can apply this truth in my life.

_____

_____

_____

_____

_____

_____

_____

This is my prayer for today.

_____

_____

_____

_____

_____

_____

What did God do in my life this week?

What is my testimony of God's work this past week? What did the Holy Spirit say to me? What prayers were answered? Who did you share Christ with? What good thing can I thank God for? Write out the difference this week made in your life.

_____

_____

_____

_____

_____

_____

_____

_____

_____

_____

_____

_____

_____

Why We Believe the Bible is God's Word

VIDEO NOTES

_____

_____

_____

_____

_____

_____

WARM UP

1. You've heard the term "fake news" recently in the press. How do you tell if it is fake news or real?

2. Which do you like better, a physical Bible that is like a book, or a digital Bible on your tablet or phone? Why?

3. Do you remember the days when you first started reading and hearing God's word, the Bible? What was it like for you?

"Jesus answered, 'It is written, Man shall not live on bread alone, but on every word that comes from the mouth of God.'" (Matthew 4:4)

Week Three Big Idea:

Is it really intelligent thinking to believe that the Bible could be God's Word?

The Bible is an amazing, one-of-a -kind piece of literature. It is the best-selling book of all time with over five billion copies sold and distributed.

But even though the Bible is so accessible and so many people own a copy, there is still confusion about the authority of the Bible and how it impacts our lives. Have you ever wondered if the Bible is really inspired by God, or is it just the writings of a few zealous men? Is it really relevant for today, or just an ancient religious manuscript? And most importantly, can we really trust a 2000-year-old book to give direction to our lives today? I believe we can do just that!

Reason #1 – The Bible declares it is God's word

The Bible is the only book that makes the claim to be the very Word of God. That is a pretty bold statement. But, the facts are there to be reckoned with. The Bible backs up that bold statement with these two truths:

1. It is God-breathed

"All Scripture is inspired by God and is useful to teach us what is true…" (2 Tim. 3:13 NLT)

The word "inspired" is the Greek word "*theopneustos*" which means "God-breathed." It is the very breath of God. Although it is true that men wrote the manuscripts and human fingerprints are evident, every part of the Bible is the product of the exhalation of God Himself.

It is incredible to think that the God who created the universe and all its wonders really wants to know you personally and have a relationship with you...up close and personal. The Bible is God's very breath and His own love letter to you, His child.

2. It is living and active

"For the word of God is living and active and sharper than any two-edged sword piercing to the division of soul and spirit, joints and of marrow, and discerning the thoughts and intention of the heart." (Hebrews 4:12 NASB)

The Bible is alive and powerful, and amazingly, God can be personally known and experienced through reading it. What other book do you know of that can make that astonishing claim?

Have you ever read a verse in the Bible, and it came alive in your spirit? Can you remember the verse and what it was like?

_____

_____

_____

Reason #2 – It is a supernatural work

The accuracy of the Bible proves it is a document with divine design. When you look at the Bible's unity, structure, and subject matter, it is undoubtedly a supernatural work. Its writing was nothing short of miraculous! Maybe you have never thought about it before, but the Bible is like no other book. It was produced in the most unusual way.

The Bible was written:
- By forty different authors
- Representing twenty different occupations
- Living in ten countries
- During a fifteen-hundred-year span
- Working in three languages.
- The authors produced sixty-six books expressing every form of writing from poetry to history.

Have you read much of the Bible, or the entire Bible? Do you have a regular Bible reading plan?

_____

_____

Reason #3 – The characters are authentic

I love how the characters in the Bible are so relatable. They are just like us. There is a real sense of authenticity to the scriptures with which we can identify. They were not perfect. They were ordinary people just like you and me who were transformed from the inside out.

- Abraham had a problem with lying.
- Moses had severe insecurity issues.
- David had a problem with lust.
- Peter had a foul mouth and a problem with betrayal.
...and the list goes on....

It is all there for us to see. The Bible does not try to hide people behind a mask of perfection. We get to see the good, the bad, and the ugly. But, most importantly, we get to see their lives transformed by the power of God.

Is there a person in the Bible to whom you can relate? Perhaps Peter, Thomas, Mary, or Martha?

Reason #4 - Jesus believed the Bible was God's word

Jesus is the greatest expert witness on the Bible. When confronted by the religious elite about the most controversial doctrine of his day- the resurrection- Jesus quoted them a passage from the Old Testament saying,

> "You are in error because you do not know the Scriptures or the power of God. At the resurrection people will neither marry not be given in marriage, they will be like the angels in heaven. But about the resurrection of the dead-have you not read what God said to you, 'I am the God of Abraham, the God of Isaac, and the God of Jacob'? He is not the God of the dead but of the living." (Matthew 22:29-32)

Jesus used "I am" instead of saying "I was". In other words, Abraham, Isaac, and Jacob are still alive, just not on the earth. In a very simple statement, Jesus proved the resurrection on the tense of a verb. If Jesus used Scripture and believed it to be the very words of God then why would we ever feel embarrassed about believing it too.

Conclusion

The Bible is an amazing, one-of-a-kind, God-breathed, living, and active book. I know of no other decision that will make a bigger impact in your life than being confident the Bible is the Word of God.

APPLICATION

1. What are your biggest issues with the Bible? Have you ever questioned its credibility?

2. Discuss the various ways or reading and studying the Bible. Share how each person approaches their own personal reading plan.

PRAYER

1. Pray for each other to be deeply grounded in God's word, promises, and blessings.

2. Take the time to discuss and pray about specific challenges groups member may have, and find a promise of God's word to stand on.

3. Pray for each member of the group to have the opportunity to share what they learned from this lesson with someone outside the group.

Digging Deeper

Bible Study Methods[3]

Below is information provided that will present 12 proven Bible study methods that will enable you to study the Bible on your own. They are given in the order of simplicity and use of reference tools, beginning with the easiest and moving on to the harder ones.

1. **The Devotional Method.**
   Select a short portion of your Bible and prayerfully meditate on it till the Holy Spirit shows you a way to apply the truth to your life. Write out a personal application.

2. **The Chapter Summary Method.**
   Read a chapter of a Bible book through at least five times; then write down a summary of the central thoughts you find in it.

3. **The Character Quality Method.**
   Choose a character quality you would like to work on in your life and study what the Bible says about it.

4. **The Thematic Method.**
   Select a Bible theme to study. Then think of three to five questions you'd like to have answered about that theme. Next study all the references you can find on your theme and record the answers to your questions.

5. **The Biographical Method.**
   Select a Bible character and research all the verses about that person in order to study his life and characteristics. Make notes on his attitudes, strengths, and weaknesses. Then apply what you have learned to your own life.

---

[3] Bible Study Methods, Rick Warren, Zondervan, 1981

6. **The Topical Method.**
   Collect and compare all the verses you can find on a particular topic. Organize your conclusions into an outline that you can share with another person.

7. **The Word Study Method.**
   Study the important words of the Bible. Find out how many times a word occurs in Scripture and how it is used. Find out the original meaning of the word.

8. **The Book Background Method.**
   Study how history, geography, culture, science, and politics affected what happened in Bible times. Use Bible reference books to increase your understanding of the Word.

9. **The Book Survey Method.**
   Survey an entire book of the Bible by reading it through several times to get a general overview of its contents. Study the background of the book and make notes on its contents.

10. **The Chapter Analysis Method.**
    Master the contents of a chapter of a book of the Bible by taking an in-depth look at each verse in that chapter. Tear each verse apart word by word, observing every detail.

11. **The Book Synthesis Method**.
    Summarize the contents and main themes of a book of the Bible after you have read it through several times. Make an outline of the book. This method is done after you have used a Book Survey Method and the Chapter Analysis Method on every chapter of that book.

12. **The Verse-by-Verse Analysis Method.**
    Select one passage of Scripture and examine it in detail by asking questions, finding cross-references, and paraphrasing each verse. Record a possible application of each verse you study.

Can we trust the Bible?[4]

It's no secret that the Bible is old. It has been around for centuries and has had a profound influence on mankind all throughout history. How do we know that the copies we have today are an accurate representation of the original manuscripts?

> *"We do not have the original manuscripts of the Bible. The originals are lost. We don't know when and we don't know by whom. What we have are copies of copies. In some instances, the copies we have are twentieth generation copies."*
>
> C. J. Werleman, *Jesus Lied, Pg 41*

In today's world the integrity of the Bible is in question. People use to ask, "Is it true?" But now they ask, "Is that what the Bible really said?"

I want to give you four reasons for confidence in the scriptures.

So, do we still have the original manuscripts of the New Testaments? No, we do not. These original manuscripts, written on fragile papyri, the ancient world's paper, were handed over and over again by ancient scribes who handled them all the way up to perhaps the second century so many times that the papyri would have worn out. Now this may sound alarming, but it does not make the Bible untrustworthy.

If we want to understand New Testament reliability, there are four questions we need to ask.

---

[4] **Daniel B. Wallace**
Executive Director for the Study of New Testament Manuscripts.
https://www.youtube.com/watch?v=II492D9Fj4c

Question 1 – How many textual variants are there?

Textual Variants – where manuscripts have differences in word order, omission/addition of words, spelling, etc.

There are about 140,000 words in the Greek New Testament. And the best estimate today is there are 500,000 textural variants, or a little over 3.5 variants per word in the Greek New Testament. Now these numbers seem astronomical when considering these ancient manuscripts, but let's talk about two key factors: quantity and time. The reason that we have a lot of textual variants is because we have a lot of manuscripts. Consider other ancient authors. The average classical Greek writer has less than 15 copies of his works still in existence. And if you were to stack them up they would be no more than four feet high. The earliest copies of their works typically date more than half a millennium after they were written. Consider now the New Testament manuscripts. The earliest manuscripts are only decades from the originals. And if you were to stack every copy of every New Testament manuscript that we have on top of each other it would be more than 1.25 miles high. So, if we are going to be skeptical about the New Testament, and if we applied that same skepticism to other ancient Greco Roman literature, we would be plunged right back into the dark ages.

Question 2 - What kinds of variant are there?

Of the 500,000 or so variants that we have, more than 99% of them make no difference at all. If a word is spelled incorrectly that counts as a variant, but there were no dictionaries in the ancient world and words would be spelled in a variety of ways, even by the same author many times. Word order also in Greek is a matter of emphasis rather a manner of meaning like it is in English because Greek is a highly inflected language. So, you can change the word order without changing the meaning. What we need to focus on are the one-fifth of one percent of

REASONS For HOPE | 69

the textual variants that actually affect things. This group is both meaningful and viable.

A meaningful variant impacts the meaning of the text/passage. A viable variant has the possibility of being traced back to the original manuscript.

For example, in Mark chapter 9, Jesus is telling his disciples why they couldn't cast out a particular demon. He said, this kind of demon can only come out by prayer. Other manuscripts we've found finish the verse by adding the phrase, "and fasting". This variant has implications on Christian practice, but not on doctrine. It's important, but it's not that important.

Question 3 – What theological beliefs depend on textually suspect passages?

When examining the deity of Christ, we understand the claims that Jesus is God. But Dan Brown argues in the DaVinci Code that this belief originated from the Emperor Constantine at the Counsel of Nicea in A.D. 325. Well, look at the evidence. The papyri known as P66, which is a manuscript of John's gospel and dated about 150 years prior to the Counsel of Nicea, clears this issue off the table with its affirmation of Jesus' deity in chapter one. In fact, there is not a single manuscript, in any language, written at any time that denies the deity of Jesus in John 1:1. What about other Christian beliefs? What about His virgin birth? What about the resurrection? Was Jesus really raised from the dead? Does the New Testament actually affirm that? Even though some manuscripts may not affirm those doctrines in every single place, we have no manuscript that has any credibility to it that denies any essential Christian belief.

Question 4- Is the Bible we have today what they wrote then?

In all particulars, we don't know. It's probably not identical.   But in all essentials – yes! What we have today in all essentials is the very word of God. No essential Christian belief is jeopardized by any viable variant.

Daniel B. Wallace
Executive Director for the Study of New Testament Manuscripts.
https://www.youtube.com/watch?v=II492D9Fj4c

Notes

Daily Devotional– Day 15

"The entrance of Your words gives light; It gives understanding to the simple." (Psalm 119:130 NKJV)

Have you ever experienced deep darkness? I mean, darkness so thick that you can't see your hand in front of you? There are some caves around the world where this type of darkness gives people a scary, and sometimes frightful, chill.

Have you ever experienced darkness of soul? This is the type of darkness where fear grips you, where all seems lost. You are without hope, direction, confidence, and you are completely and utterly lost. There are many people around us who live such lives. They are depressed, full of anxiety and fear. Life is dark and many times can end in disaster.

The good news of this promise today is God's word brings light. It can shine in the darkness. It can bring hope to the hopeless. It can bring comfort to the downcast. Yes, God's word, when read, meditated upon, and believed, can bring light into a dark soul and give hope, salvation, healing, and direction.

So today ask yourself if there is any darkness surrounding your life. Where do you need light, direction, encouragement, or hope? Take the time to find a promise of God that brings light, and let God shine upon the darkness.

This is what today's verse means to me.

_____

_____

_____

_____

_____

_____

Here is how I can apply this truth in my life.

_____

_____

_____

_____

_____

This is my prayer for today.

_____

_____

_____

_____

Daily Devotional– Day 16

"My son, give attention to my words; Incline your ear to my sayings. Do not let them depart from your eyes; Keep them in the midst of your heart; For they are life to those who find them, and health to all their flesh." (Proverbs 4:20ff)

When was the last time you had something very important to take care of in your life? When was the last time you had a dead-line to meet, or a very important meeting to keep? At times, we all have important tasks, obligations, and life assignments that we must fulfill and keep. But there is one assignment, task, and meeting that is perhaps more vital than them all, and that is the appointment you have with God's word.

In today's verse, notice the phrases "give attention to", "incline", and "keep them". These words give us a sense of urgency, obligation, and responsibility to pay attention to God's word. Why? Because His words are life and health. Yes, as we place God's word as the number priority above all we do in life, then His promise is to bring life in all we do.

So today, make God's word in your life a priority. Don't allow other facets of life crowd out your time with the Lord and Him speaking to you through His word.

This is what today's verse means to me.

_____

_____

_____

_____

_____

Here is how I can apply this truth in my life.

_____

_____

_____

_____

_____

This is my prayer for today.

_____

_____

_____

_____

_____

_____

Daily Devotional– Day 17

"So shall My word be that goes forth from My mouth; It shall not return to Me void, but it shall accomplish what I please, And it shall prosper in the thing for which I sent it." (Isaiah 55:11 NKJV)

Has anyone every made a promise to you but failed to keep it? Sure, we've all had politicians, parents, co-workers, or friends who have at one time or another made a promise, but their words ended up empty, without meaning, and being, well, just words.

It is the rare individual who can keep 100% of their promises and commitments. In fact, it's impossible. Why? Because we're fallible and make mistakes.

What about God? Can His word be trusted? Absolutely! We're told today by Isaiah that God's word will accomplish what He pleases. Further, His word prospers and brings about what He promised. What this means to you is that contained in every word of God is the power of God to bring about what He says. This means you can lay claim to one of His 7, 487 promises and know He will stand behind His word to fulfill it in your life. So today, find a promise, believe it, praise God for it, and then step back and know He will fulfill it – AMEN.

This is what today's verse means to me.

_____

_____

_____

_____

_____

_____

Here is how I can apply this truth in my life.

_____

_____

_____

_____

_____

This is my prayer for today.

_____

_____

_____

_____

_____

Daily Devotional– Day 18

"God is not a man, that He should lie, nor a son of man, that He should repent. Has He said, and will He not do? Or has He spoken, and will He not make it good?" (Numbers 23:19 NKJV)

Many times in life, there will be instances when our faith is challenged by circumstances outside of our control. Some will battle sickness. Many people will experience loss, whether it be financially, relationally, or in business.

But through whatever we face in life, there is a rock we can stand upon with the knowledge that, with God, we cannot fail. Why? Because when God says something, we can rest assured that He will make it good.

What this means to you today is God will not lie to you. He cannot lie. He speaks, and it is truth that will not change, alter, or deviate. Further, when God's word is believed and received, what He said He will do, He'll do. So, what do you need God to do in your life today? Take the time to turn your attention to what He has said about your life and know that He has spoken and will stand behind His word to make it good in your life. He promises peace, abundance, rest, strength, healing, and provision. Go read Jeremiah 29:11, Phil 4:13, and Mark 11:23, and believe every word!

This is what today's verse means to me.

_____

_____

Here is how I can apply this truth in my life.

_____

_____

_____

_____

_____

This is my prayer for today.

_____

_____

_____

_____

_____

_____

Daily Devotional– Day 19

"So now, brethren, I commend you to God and to the word of His grace, which is able to build you up and give you an inheritance among all those who are sanctified." (Acts 20:32 NKJV)

When was the last time you felt really weak? Was it because of the flu or cold? Were you exhausted because of other emotional battles or challenges?   Or were you discouraged because of some bad news, disheartening information, or a letdown?

Notice today's verse gives you two promises. The first is God's promise to build you up. This speaks of lifting you up out of a state of weakness and bringing you into strength. God's word will build you up, make you strong, and bring strength to your soul. The second promise is to give you an inheritance. Yes, you have an inheritance of abundance in the Kingdom of Heaven. Whatever need you have or will ever have has already been provided for you and all of us through Jesus Christ. The Bible says we have been blessed with all spiritual blessing in Christ (Eph. 1:3).

So today, spend time in God's word. Meditate on it, pray it, proclaim it, and believe it. As you do, His promise to you is to build you up, and make you strong, confident, and bold. And in so doing, you'll again know that His inheritance is available and yours today!

This is what today's verse means to me.

_____

_____

_____

_____

_____

_____

Here is how I can apply this truth in my life.

_____

_____

_____

_____

_____

This is my prayer for today.

_____

_____

_____

_____

_____

Daily Devotional– Day 20

"So then faith comes by hearing, and hearing by the word of God." (Romans 10:17 NKJV)

There is a lot of negative, depressing, and discouraging news running through the airwaves and internet every day. It can be depressing if each day we focus our lives on what's happening around the world with the political confusions, wars, violence, and distress.

As believers we have another source of information to live by and base our lives on. We have a source of strength and faith from Heaven that will fill your heart with a bold and audacious faith. Yes, God's word has the power to radically change your life from weakness to strength, from fear to faith, from poverty to abundance, and from hopelessness to a clear and bright future.

But first, you must take the time to allow God's word to penetrate your mind and soul so that His word can cause faith to rise to a new level. We're told this kind of faith comes as we hear God's word. There is a literal transformation that takes place when God's word saturates your soul and eradicates fears. Do you need more faith? Then get more of God's word in your life. Everyday, take the time to fill your faith tank with God's word and see what will happen in your life.

This is what today's verse means to me.

_____

_____

_____

_____

_____

_____

Here is how I can apply this truth in my life.

_____

_____

_____

_____

_____

This is my prayer for today.

_____

_____

_____

_____

_____

_____

Daily Devotional– Day 21

"You shall know the truth, and the truth shall make you free."
(John 8:32 NKJV)

We live in a free county. Many freedoms are afforded to us in everyday life. We are free to come and go as we please. We are free to buy and sell, travel, and do pretty much whatever we'd like to do, within the law.

But even with the freedom we have as a nation, there are thousands of individuals living in bondage. Many live in bondage to their past hurts and abuse. Many live in poverty and lack, sickness and disease, and fear and failure.

The good news of Jesus Christ is that freedom is available to any and all. Yes, true freedom from all bondages, fears, guilt, and shame is yours. But this freedom comes as we know His truth, for His truth will set us free. It is as we hear God's truth that we discover we don't have to live in bondage to anything anymore. So today, is there anything that is holding you down, bringing you into lack, or causing you to despair? Then know this: God's truth is designed to bring you freedom. It's already yours because of the work of Jesus Christ, His cross, and resurrection. Believe it, confess it, and boldly proclaim that you are free in Jesus name!

This is what today's verse means to me.

_____

_____

_____

Here is how I can apply this truth in my life.

_____

_____

_____

_____

_____

This is my prayer for today.

_____

_____

_____

_____

_____

What did God do in my life this week?

What is my testimony of God's work this past week? What did the Holy Spirit say to me? What prayers were answered? Who did you share Christ with? What good thing can I thank God for? Write out the difference this week made in your life.

_____

_____

_____

_____

_____

_____

_____

_____

_____

_____

_____

_____

Week Four
Settle it Once and for All
Why We Believe the Bible is God's Words – Part 2

_____

_____

_____

_____

_____

_____

WARM UP

1. Are you a morning person, or an evening person? Is it easier for you to read God's word in the morning or at night?

2. Do you have a favorite book of the Bible? How about a favorite person in the Bible you identify with?

3. What is your greatest challenge in reading and memorizing the Bible?

"The grass withers, the flower fades, but the Word of our God stands forever." (Isiah 40:8 NLT)

Week Four Big Idea:

Can we really believe that the Bible is true and that the God who created the universe actually speaks through a book?

In our scripture for this week, the prophet Isaiah states that God's word stands forever. It is eternal, unshakable, and it can be trusted. Last week we discovered four reasons why the Bible really is God's Word. This week, we will dig a little deeper to uncover three more reasons why the Bible can be trusted and give us hope for our lives.

Reason #5 – Numerous prophecies have been fulfilled

Prophecy (something said in advance that later happened) is powerful evidence that the Bible is God's Word. J. Barton Payne's Encyclopedia of Biblical Prophecy lists 1,239 prophecies in the Old Testament and 578 prophecies in the New Testament, for a total of 1,817. These encompass 8,352 verses. Fulfilled prophecy sets the Bible apart from all other religious writings and is one of the strongest proofs that the Bible is God's Word.

Prophecy is one of God's litmus tests that He uses to prove He is who He says He is. It is uncanny that one hundred percent of the time, God accurately predicts what will happen before it happens.

God spoke through the prophet Isaiah saying,

"Remember the former things, those of long ago; I am God, and there is no other; I am God, and there is none like me. I make known the end from the beginning, from ancient times, what is

still to come. I say, 'My purpose will stand, and I will do all that I please.'" (Isaiah 46:9-10 NLT)

Notice that God said, "My purpose (my Word) will stand, and I will do all that I please." The Bible is an ancient writing, but it is still powerful and relevant, and we are still seeing prophecy fulfilled in our present day. Amazing!

The most astounding prophecies are about Christ. There are over three hundred specific prophecies of Jesus' first coming.

These are just 5 of the 300 prophecies about Jesus taken from the book of Isaiah:
1. He would be born of a virgin (Isa. 7:14).
2. He would be from the house of David (Isa.11:10).
3. There would be one who would prepare the way (Isa. 40:3-5).
4. He would be anointed with the Holy Spirit (Isa. 11:2).
5. He would be crucified with transgressors (Isa. 53:12).

Why do you suppose God focused so much of the Bible on prophecies regarding His Son Jesus Christ?

_____

_____

_____

Reason #6 – The Bible has been accurately transmitted

The Bible's accuracy and purity as it was passed down through the centuries is nothing short of miraculous.

Whenever a story is retold again and again there is usually some slight embellishment or addition to the storyline. Take the kid's game "telephone". By the time the sentence is whispered eight or nine times it, is never what it started out to be. It always changes in the retelling.

Maybe you have wondered, can a Bible that has been copied so many times for so many hundreds of years really be accurate? It is interesting to note that many hold the works of Homer, who lived in 900 BC, and is famous for writing *The Iliad* and *The Odyssey,* to be completely authentic. Our earliest copy of his work is dated 400 BC. That is a span of about five hundred years between the time he lived and our earliest copies.

The New Testament was written between AD 40 and AD 100 and the earliest copy is from AD 125. That is only a twenty-five-year difference. During that period there were still people living who could authenticate the text. The Bible is the most accurately transmitted ancient document known to man. The Dead Sea Scrolls also support the accuracy of the Bible in that they contain thousands of texts that reveal the Old Testament was not degraded over time.

God spoke the Word, it was copied, and then passed along to us today. In fact, it is the same text that people read over two thousand years ago, and it is still just as powerful!

Has anyone ever challenged you stating the Bible is a mere book written by man and can't be trusted? What can you now say?

_____

_____

_____

_____

Reason #7 – The Bible has real impact on lives

The Bible is more than words; it is an active force. The Word of God is able to transform lives and nations. When God's Word is applied, it brings life, health, and real change. Where the Bible is believed and lived out, women become persons instead of property, equal rights and justice are championed, slavery is abolished, dignity is restored to humanity, and people of all race, gender, and economic status are loved and fulfilled.

> *"Do not conform to the pattern of this world, but be transformed by the renewing of your mind. Then you will be able to test and approve what God's will is - His good, pleasing, and perfect will."*
> *Romans 12:2 (NLT)*

The Bible contains God's will for our lives, and it is good, pleasing, and perfect. The Bible is God's love letter to us, His children, and it is meant to bless and enrich our lives by showing us a better way to live. Jesus promised that if we would apply the truths of God's Word to our lives, we could truly be free.

> *"Then you will know the truth, and the truth will set you free."*
> *John 8:32 (NLT)*

How has the Bible impacted your life since coming to know Jesus Christ?

_____

_____

_____

Conclusion

The truths in Scripture always bring us to a crossroad where we must make an intelligent decision about what we believe.

Now, it is time for you to settle once and for all that the Bible truly is the Word of God. Coming to a solid conviction about the Bible will be a turning point in your life. Your faith must move from beliefs to convictions. The Bible is the unshakable Word of God, our reason for hope, and it will stand forever.

APPLICATION

1. What is the strongest evidence to you that God's word, the Bible, is real?

2. Share with each other a promise of God's word that you've experienced coming true.

3. Talk about any further questions, doubts, or challenges the group members may have in God's word and how best to answer those.

PRAYER

1. Pray for each group member to know and receive the power of God's promises for whatever need they may have in their life.

2. Pray for each group member to take courage and overcome any doubts or fears they may be facing.

3. Pray for each member of the group to have the opportunity to share God's word and promises with someone else in their coming week. Remember, Jesus said, "You are the light of the world".

Digging Deeper

Statistical probability of fulfilling prophecies

A well-known professor and mathematician tried to calculate the probability of any one man fulfilling eight prophecies. He finally came to the conclusion that it would be one in ten to the seventeenth power. To make that easier to grasp, it would be like covering the entire state of Texas in silver dollars two feet deep. Pretty unlikely, right? Well, Jesus didn't fulfill eight prophecies concerning himself, but three hundred. Fulfilled prophecy is one of the strongest evidences that the Bible is God's Word and that we can trust what it says.

Here are just eight of the prophecies fulfilled in Jesus Christ at His crucifixion.[5]

Bible Prophecy: Isaiah 53:3 says, "He was despised and rejected by men, a man of sorrows, and familiar with suffering. Like one from whom men hide their faces He was despised, and we esteemed Him not."
Fulfillment: John 1:10-11 says, "He was in the world, and though the world was made through Him, the world did not recognize Him. He came to that which was His own, but His own did not receive Him."

Bible Prophecy: Psalm 41:9 says, "Even my close friend, whom I trusted, he who shared my bread, has lifted up his heel against me."
Fulfillment: Mark 14:10 says, "Then Judas Iscariot, one of the Twelve, went to the chief priests to betray Jesus to them."

---

[5] **All About Jesus Christ**
https://www.allaboutjesuschrist.org/prophecies-fulfilled-by-the-crucifixion-of-jesus-christ-faq.htm

Bible Prophecy: Zechariah 11:12 says, "I told them, 'If you think it best, give me my pay; but if not, keep it.' So they paid me thirty pieces of silver."

Fulfillment: Matthew 26:14-16 says, "Then one of the Twelve - the one called Judas Iscariot - went to the chief priests and asked, 'What are you willing to give me if I hand him over to you?' So they counted out for him thirty silver coins."

Bible Prophecy: Isaiah 53:7 says, "He was oppressed and afflicted, yet He did not open his mouth; He was led like a lamb to the slaughter, and as a sheep before her shearers is silent, so He did not open his mouth."

Fulfillment: Mark 15:5 says, "But Jesus still made no reply, and Pilate was amazed."

Bible Prophecy: Psalm 22:1-2 says, "My God, my God, why have you forsaken me? Why are you so far from saving me, so far from the words of my groaning? O my God, I cry out by day, but you do not answer, by night, and am not silent."

Fulfillment: Matthew 27:46 says, "About the ninth hour Jesus cried out in a loud voice, 'Eloi, Eloi, lama sabachthani?' - which means, 'My God, my God, why have you forsaken me?'"

Bible Prophecy: Psalm 22:7-8 says, "All who see me mock me; they hurl insults, shaking their heads: 'He trusts in the LORD; let the LORD rescue him. Let him deliver him, since he delights in him.'"

Fulfillment: Matthew 27:41-44 says, "In the same way the chief priests, the teachers of the law, and the elders mocked him. 'He saved others,' they said, 'but he can't save himself! He's the King of Israel! Let him come down now from the cross, and we will believe in him. He trusts in God. Let God rescue him now if he wants him, for he said, I am the Son of God.' In the same way the robbers who were crucified with him also heaped insults on him."

Bible Prophecy: Psalm 22:15 says, "My strength is dried up like a potsherd, and my tongue sticks to the roof of my mouth; you lay me in the dust of death."

Fulfillment: Matthew 27:48 says, "Immediately one of them ran and got a sponge. He filled it with wine vinegar, put it on a stick, and offered it to Jesus to drink."

Bible Prophecy: Psalm 22:17-18 says, "I can count all my bones; people stare and gloat over me. They divide my garments among them and cast lots for my clothing."

Fulfillment: John 19:23 says, "When the soldiers crucified Jesus, they took his clothes, dividing them into four shares, one for each of them, with the undergarment remaining. This garment was seamless, woven in one piece from top to bottom."

Jesus quotes the Old Testament

Here is a list of the references to the Old Testament from the lips of Jesus Christ. This list further validates the validity of the Old Testament and its influence in Jesus' ministry. A great study would be to look up and highlight all these references in the Old Testament as words of Jesus.

1. Turning a rock into bread - Matthew 4:4 from Deuteronomy 8:3

2. Jumping off the top of the temple - Matthew 4:7 from Deut. 6:16

3. Worship only the Lord God – Matthew 4:10 from Deut. 6:13

4. Regarding murder – Matthew 5:21 from Exodus 20:13

5. Regarding adultery – Matthew 5:27 from Exodus 20:14

6. Regarding divorce – Matthew 5:31 from Deut. 24:1

7. Bearing false witness – Matthew 5:33 from Numbers 30:2

8. Turning the other cheek – Matthew 5:38 from Exodus 21:23-25

9. Honoring parents– Matthew 15:1-6 from Exodus 20:12

10. Divorce and creation - Matthew 19:4-6 from Genesis 1:27 and 2:24

11. Ten Commandments – Matthew 19:17-20 from Exodus 20:12-16

12. The resurrection from the dead – Matt. 22:31-32 from Exodus 3:6

13. The two greatest commandments – Matthew 22:37 from Deut. 6:5

14. The testimony of two – John 8:12-13 from Deut. 17:6

15. Jesus reads from the Isaiah - Luke 4:17-19 from Isaiah 61:1-2

16. The centrality of mercy – Matthew 9:13 from Hosea 6:6

17. The pains of the messianic age – Matthew 10:35-36 from Micah 7:6

18. The messenger arrives – Matthew 11:10 from Malachi 3:1

19. Hearing but not understanding – Matt. 13:14-15 from Isaiah 6:9-10

20. True and false honor – Matthew 15:7 from Isaiah 29:13

21. House of prayer – Matt 21:13 from Isaiah 56:7 and Jeremiah 7:11

22. Shepherd and sheep – Matthew 26:31 from Zechariah 13:7

23. Counted as a criminal – Luke 22:37 from Isaiah 52:13-53:12

24. God and His students – John 6:45 from Isaiah 54:13

25. Out of the mouths of babes – Matthew 21:16 from Psalm 8

26. Unexpected cornerstone – Matthew 21:42 from Psalm 118:22-23

27. The Lord to the Lord - Matthew 22:43-44 from Psalm 110

28. When redemption happens – Matthew 23:37-39 from Psalm 118

29. Abomination of desolation – Matt. 24:15-16 from Daniel 9:27, 11:31

30. God and the Son of God –John 10:22 from Psalm 82:6-7

31. Betrayal by a friend – John 13:18 from Psalm 41:9

32. Baseless hatred – John 15:25 from Psalm 35:19

33. A psalm from the cross – Matthew 27:46 from Psalm 22:1

Notes

Daily Devotional– Day 22

"Your word is a lamp to my feet and a light to my path." (Psalm 119:105 NKJV)

Have you ever been lost? Perhaps you've been out hiking, or driving in a new city, and the sense of being lost overwhelms you? Or, how about having the sense of being lost without a sense of direction or purpose in life? We've all been there at one time or another. We've looked for an answer, direction, or a solution to a life challenge.

We're told in today's verse that God's word is a lamp and light. It is God's word which gives direction in darkness, guidance when hopelessness comes, and an answer when we need a path to walk on when life gets dark.

Are you looking for direction, support, answers, or a road map for life? Then get out God's GPS, His word, and keep God's word in your life as the final authority for everything you do. In so doing, you'll find answers, direction, purpose, God's promises, and a path to walk on as you live out your Christian life. Read God's word, and let it shine light in your darkness.

This is what today's verse means to me.

_____

_____

_____

_____

_____

Here is how I can apply this truth in my life.

_____

_____

_____

_____

_____

_____

This is my prayer for today.

_____

_____

_____

_____

_____

_____

_____

Daily Devotional– Day 23

"If you abide in Me, and My words abide in you, you will ask what you desire, and it shall be done for you". (John 15:7 NKJV)

This is one of the most powerful, encouraging, and faith-filled promises in the Bible. Is Jesus saying that we can truly ask for what we desire and He'll do it for us? Read the verse again; that's what it says, friend. You can ask what for what you desire and Jesus will do it for you.

But notice before this wonderful promise Jesus conditioned our asking by our devotion to and abiding in His word. The condition for our asking is based upon our first being filled with and connected to God's word. It is His word that fills us, gives us faith, and changes our attitudes, motivation, and life priorities. As we abide in His word, God's desires become our desires; we then pray His desires and He fulfills them.

So today, make a fresh commitment to abide, read, meditate, and fully commit to living God's word. As you do, you then can ask whatever you desire and His promise is to answer your prayer. AMEN!

This is what today's verse means to me.

_____

_____

_____

_____

_____

Here is how I can apply this truth in my life.

_____

_____

_____

_____

_____

_____

This is my prayer for today.

_____

_____

_____

_____

_____

_____

_____

Daily Devotional– Day 24

"When you received the word of God which you heard from us, you welcomed it not as the word of men, but as it is in truth, the word of God, which also effectively works in you who believe." (1 Thes. 2:13 NKJV)

Throughout history people have sought for ways to change their life. Today much money is spent on changing and modifying the human body through surgery. People spend thousands on self-help books to deal with depression and all sorts of emotional challenges. Countless hours are spent in the gym to get the physique and body like the ones in the glamour magazine.

But truly the only source of lasting change is God's word. His word has the power to *"effectively work"* in you in every area of life. God's word can dig deep into your soul and bring true peace, love, and forgiveness where no other source can. God's word can and will change, heal, renew, and bring hope as give yourself to the study, prayer, and living out of His truth. Thank God today for His word having the power to change you and work in you. Believe it – AMEN!

This is what today's verse means to me.

Here is how I can apply this truth in my life.

_____

_____

_____

_____

_____

_____

This is my prayer for today.

_____

_____

_____

_____

_____

_____

_____

_____

Daily Devotional– Day 25

"For the word of God is living and powerful, and sharper than any two-edged sword, piercing even to the division of soul and spirit, and of joints and marrow, and is a discerner of the thoughts and intents of the heart." (Hebrews 4:12 NKJV)

There is something supernatural about God's word. In the beginning He created the heavens and earth with His word. God spoke and life began. God speaks and creation takes place. God's word is alive, powerful, and is the only word that carries within itself the creative ability to fulfill that which was spoken.

When you, as a believer in Christ, read, hear, and believe God's word, creative power enters your soul and begins to bring life, faith, and the power to fulfill God's promises in your life. God's word is living. It is like a sword. God's word divides right from wrong and exposes the thoughts and motives of your heart.

Do you need hope, victory, and blessing in your life? Take the time to fill your life with God's word. As you read and meditate on God's word, the power to create and change enters your heart and soul and brings about what His word promises you. Believe it - AMEN

This is what today's verse means to me.

_____

_____

_____

_____

_____

_____

Here is how I can apply this truth in my life.

_____

_____

_____

_____

_____

This is my prayer for today.

_____

_____

_____

_____

_____

_____

Daily Devotional– Day 26

"The words that I speak to you are spirit, and they are life." (John 6:63 NKJV)

God's word is more than ink on a paper, a good story in a book, or just another man's opinion. God's words contain life. That is, God's word has the power to bring life whenever it is believed and received. God's word entering a sick body can bring healing. God's word can change a life filled with fear and doubt into one filled with courage and faith. A person in poverty or lack, when they discover the life of God's word, can be transformed into blessing, provision, and abundance.

The priority for every believer is to make God's word the final authority in life. God's word can save, heal, deliver, restore, build, renew, give direction, and guidance; it opens doors, calms the soul, breaks strongholds, and fulfills His purpose and plan for your life.

Give yourself daily to reading and meditating on God's word. Make it first before any other source of information or opinion. Then choose to believe and respond to what you read. In so doing you'll find life and fulfillment of God's promises to you.

This is what today's verse means to me.

_____

_____

_____

_____

_____

Here is how I can apply this truth in my life.

_____

_____

_____

_____

_____

_____

This is my prayer for today.

_____

_____

_____

_____

_____

_____

_____

Daily Devotional– Day 27

"Blessed is the man (whose) delight is in the law of the LORD, *and in His law he meditates day and night. He shall be like a tree planted by the rivers of water, that brings forth its fruit in its season, whose leaf also shall not wither; and whatever he does shall prosper." (Psalm 1:2-3 NKJV)*

Whatever you do shall prosper! That is a powerful promise of God. Just imagine what it would be like to live a life that whatever you do, you will prosper. Is it available? Can this be true? The answer is yes! God's word promises it!

But the condition for this promise is for you to delight and meditate in God's word day and night. This means putting God's word first in all matters of life. This means taking time to read, listen to, and obey God's word. This speaks of thinking about, meditating on, and living out God's word. As you do, you'll find you too can be like that tree planted, growing and bearing fruit. You too can prosper in all you do.

So today, make a quality decision to not allow anything to take priority over your time in God's presence and His word. Make it a priority! Have a set time and place each day to dig into God's truth.

This is what today's verse means to me.

_____

_____

_____

_____

_____

_____

Here is how I can apply this truth in my life.

_____

_____

_____

_____

_____

_____

This is my prayer for today.

_____

_____

_____

_____

Daily Devotional– Day 28

"This Book of the Law shall not depart from your mouth, but you shall meditate in it day and night, that you may observe to do according to all that is written in it. For then you will make your way prosperous, and then you will have good success." (Joshua 1:8 NKJV)

Everyone wants to be a success in life. Many go about it the wrong way, with the wrong motives, and many end up empty, frustrated, and defeated. But that doesn't have to be you. No, you can discover God's way of success, and it is found in God's word. Today's verse gives you the key to stepping into God's success and the means of activating it in your life.

You're told to not let God's word depart from your mouth. This means you need to be saying, speaking, and proclaiming God's truth. You're also told in this verse to meditate in God's word continually, so that you can obey and do it. It is this commitment to God's word that positions you to become prosperous and successful. So, to the degree that you abide in God's word, you'll find true success in life. Commit to believe and obey all of God's truth today. AMEN!

This is what today's verse means to me.

_____

_____

_____

_____

Here is how I can apply this truth in my life.

This is my prayer for today.

What did God do in my life this week?

What is my testimony of God's work this past week? What did the Holy Spirit say to me? What prayers were answered? Who did you share Christ with? What good thing can I thank God for? Write out the difference this week made in your life.

_____

_____

_____

_____

_____

_____

_____

_____

_____

_____

_____

_____

Week Five

How Can We Be Sure God Loves Us?

VIDEO NOTES

_____

_____

_____

_____

_____

WARM UP

1. Do you, or have you ever, had a pet that really loved you? What was that like to you?

2. What is your favorite movie showing true love between two individuals? What was it that you saw in their love?

3. Now the tough question. Have you ever had someone who said they loved you, but ending up letting you down? Ouch!

"We have known and believed that God loves us. God is love." (1 John 4:16 GWT)

Week Five Big Idea:

We can know and believe the love that God has for us.

It is very common for people to wonder about the reality of God's love. Our broken experiences in life are often punctuated by questions like, "If God loves me, why am I suffering? Why is there such injustice in the world?" Even among those who love and believe in God, it is common to face internal struggles with that belief in our hearts.

In this study, we provide a biblical and rational foundation for being sure that God is love, and that He wholeheartedly loves each and every one of us.

"Consider the kind of extravagant love the Father has lavished on us—He calls us children of God! It's true; we are His beloved children." (1 John 3:1 TVT)

Knowing that Almighty God loves us changes absolutely everything about our lives. Do you KNOW God the Father loves you? Let's consider the extravagant love of God in the following points.

1. We know God loves us because He created us.

"When I consider your heavens, the work of your fingers, the moon and the stars, which you have set in place, what is mankind that you are mindful of them, human beings that you care for them?" (Psalm 8:3-4)

Why would Almighty God love those who are sinful, selfish, and weak like us? It doesn't make sense. David considered the same question in the verse above. But God created us, as David points out. We are "the work of His fingers!" As a Creator, God took the time to craft each of us with love. If God put such thought into our creation, He surely loves us. We know God loves us because every artist loves their created work.

God created you and desires to love you. Why is it that God created you and made you a part of His plan?

_____

_____

2. We know God loves us because He is good to us.

"'For I know the plans I have for you,' declares the Lord, ,plans to prosper you and not to harm you, plans to give you hope and a future." (Jeremiah 29:11)

Have you ever been suspicious when someone acts nice towards you? We may wonder about other people's intentions toward us but we can trust the intentions of God. He thinks only about blessing, helping, and healing us. No matter what we're experiencing in life, God has a plan that He is working that benefits us.

How has a loving God been good to you? Share some examples of how a loving God has blessed you.

_____

_____

_____

3. We know God loves us because Jesus died for us.

"For God so loved the world that he gave his one and only Son, that whoever believes in him shall not perish but have eternal life." (John 3:16 NKJV)

Loving us was the most expensive thing God the Father ever did. It cost Him the very life of His only Son. We may doubt a lot of things in life (politicians, empty advertisements and the like) but we can never doubt such sacrificial love!

Have you truly experienced the love of our Father God? Share with the group what it is like for you to know and receive God's love.

_____

_____

_____

4. We know God loves us because He adopted us.

"His unchanging plan has always been to adopt us into his own family by bringing us to himself through Jesus Christ. And this gave him great pleasure." (Ephesians 1:5 NLT)

Adoption is such a powerful picture of love. The adoptive parent assumes the complete and irrevocable responsibility to love and provide for a child for its lifetime. How did we become adopted by God? The Bible tells us that the God loved us so much that He arranged our adoption. By trusting in Jesus and receiving Him into our lives, we gain the right to become sons and daughters of God. So, Paul says,

"For all who are led by the Spirit of God are children of God. So you have not received a spirit that makes you fearful slaves. Instead, you received God's Spirit when he adopted you as his own children. Now we call him, 'Abba, Father.' For his Spirit joins with our spirit to affirm that we are God's children. And since we are his children, we are his heirs. In fact, together with Christ we are heirs of God's glory..." (Romans 8:14-17 NLT)

Why is it important to let the news of your adoption travel 18" from your head to your heart?

_____

_____

_____

5. We know God loves us because the Holy Spirit confirms it.

"Because you are now part of God's family, He sent the Spirit of His Son into our hearts; and the Spirit calls out, 'Abba, Father.' You no longer have to live as a slave because you are a child of God." Galatians 4:6-7 (TVT)

The moment we trust Jesus and receive Him as Lord and Savior, we are born again, adopted into God's family, AND given a massive spiritual inheritance. God's Holy Spirit is the key player in this miracle.

In the moment of our adoption, the Holy Spirit dumps an ocean of liquid love into our hearts, and our bowed heads are lifted high. We know and believe through the Holy Spirit that we are the sons and daughters of God. As Paul says, "His Spirit joins with our spirit to affirm that we are God's children."

Conclusion

Hopefully you know some people who love you. But no matter who loves you in your life, they simply cannot love you like God loves you. God loves you better than anyone has ever loved you. He created you, He's good to you, He died for you, He adopted you, and He gives the Holy Spirit to you. Knowing that Father God loves you changes everything about your life, and gives you lots of reasons for hope.

APPLICATION

1. Discuss some ways God continues to express His love to us in everyday life.

2. Discuss some of the barriers to God's love. How can one's hurts, brokenness and rejection block God's love?

PRAYER

1. Pray for a love breakthrough from Heaven for each group member.

2. Pray that all barriers and fears would be torn down and that His love overflows.

3. Pray for each group member to have the opportunity to share God's love with their family and friends this coming week.

Digging Deeper

Four Greek words for love [6]

Love as a word describes an emotion with vastly differing degrees of intensity. We can say we love ice cream and chocolate, and we can pledge our love to a husband or wife until our dying breath.

There are four unique forms of love found in the Bible. They are communicated through four Greek words: *Eros, Storge, Philia,* and *Agape.* We'll explore these different types of love characterized by romantic love, family love, brotherly love, and God's divine love. As we do, we'll discover what love really means, and how to follow Jesus Christ's command to "love one another."

What Is Eros Love in the Bible?
Eros (pronounced: AIR-ohs) is the Greek word for sensual or romantic love. The term originated from the mythological Greek goddess of love, sexual desire, physical attraction, and physical love. Even though the term is not found in the Old Testament, *Song of Solomon* vividly portrays the passion of erotic love.

What Is Storge Love in the Bible?
Storge (pronounced: STOR-jay) is a term for love in the Bible that you may not be familiar with. This Greek word describes family love, the affectionate bond that develops naturally between parents and children, and brothers and sisters. Many examples of family love are found in Scripture, such as the mutual protection among Noah and his wife, the love of Jacob for his sons, and the strong love the sisters Martha and Mary had for their brother Lazarus.

---

[6] **Jack Zavada – ThoughtCo.com**
https://www.thoughtco.com/types-of-love-in-the-bible-700177

"Love one another with brotherly affection. Outdo one another in showing honor." (Romans 12:10 ESV)

("Love" in this verse is a compound word combining Philia and Storge).

What Is Philia Love in the Bible?

Philia (pronounced: FILL-ee-uh) is the type of intimate love in the Bible that most Christians practice toward each other. This Greek term describes the powerful emotional bond seen in deep friendships. Philia is the most general type of love in Scripture, encompassing love for fellow humans, as well as care, respect, and compassion for people in need. The concept of brotherly love that unites believers is unique to Christianity.

"Finally, all of you, have unity of mind, sympathy, brotherly love, a tender heart, and a humble mind." (1 Peter 3:8 ESV)

What Is Agape Love in the Bible?

Agape (pronounced: Uh-GAH-pay) is the highest of the four types of love in the Bible. This term defines God's immeasurable, incomparable love for humankind. It is the divine love that comes from God. Agape love is perfect, unconditional, sacrificial, and pure. Jesus told His followers to love one another in the same sacrificial way He loved them. This command was new because it demanded a new kind of love, a love like His own: agape love. What would be the outcome of this kind of love? People would be able to recognize them as Jesus' disciples because of their mutual love:

"A new commandment I give to you, that you love one another: just as I have loved you, you also are to love one another. By this all people will know that you are my disciples, if you have love for one another." (John 13:34-35 ESV)

Notes

Daily Devotional– Day 29

"As the Father loved Me, I also have loved you; abide in My love."
(John 15:9 NKJV)

The Heavenly Father loved His Son, Jesus. There was and continues to be a bond of love in this Father and Son relationship that will last for eternity. The Father loved the Son before creation. The Father loved the Son when He was upon this earth. The Father continues to love the Son even in the Heavenlies.

While on the earth, Jesus received the love, protection, and comfort of the Father on a regular basis. Over 60 times in the gospel of John, Jesus refers to His Father. He speaks of the Father communicating with Him, guiding Him, helping Him, never leaving Him, and even being there when He was raised from the dead.

You too can walk in the same love relationship that Jesus did with His Father. As Jesus receives love, He gives loves. He desires for you to abide and rest in His love. As you do, you also can know the comfort, protection, guidance, and assurance that Jesus will always be with you. So today, thank God for His love. Rest in His love. Give every challenge to Him in prayer and then let Him take over every battle while you rest in Him.

This is what today's verse means to me.

_____

_____

_____

_____

_____

_____

Here is how I can apply this truth in my life.

_____

_____

_____

_____

_____

_____

This is my prayer for today.

_____

_____

_____

_____

_____

Daily Devotional– Day 30

"Though I speak with the tongues of men and of angels, but have not love, I have become sounding brass or a clanging cymbal. ² And though I have the gift of prophecy, and understand all mysteries and all knowledge, and though I have all faith, so that I could remove mountains, but have not love, I am nothing. ³ And though I bestow all my goods to feed the poor, and though I give my body to be burned but have not love, it profits me nothing." (1 Corinthians 13:1-3 NKJV)

God is love. Everything He does is through, because of, and motivated by love. We see Jesus in the gospel as the perfect example of a life lived by love. God's love is the very foundation upon which we build and live our lives. All our interactions, desires, and motives should be lived out of His love.

Today's verse highlights the priority of love. Paul gives several actions of life such as speaking, prophesying, understanding all, moving mountains, and even giving one's life as a martyr. But through it all, if it's not done in love, it is worthless, nothing, and unprofitable. So take time today to consider your life and evaluate your love walk. Everything you say and achieve must be lived out in love; otherwise all your success will be worthless.

This is what today's verse means to me.

_____

_____

_____

Here is how I can apply this truth in my life.

_____

_____

_____

_____

_____

_____

This is my prayer for today.

_____

_____

_____

_____

Daily Devotional– Day 31

"Love suffers long and is kind; love does not envy; love does not parade itself, is not puffed up; ⁵ *does not behave rudely, does not seek its own, is not provoked, thinks no evil;* ⁶ *does not rejoice in iniquity, but rejoices in the truth;* ⁷ *bears all things, believes all things, hopes all things, endures all things. Love never fails."* (1 Corinthians 13:4-8 NKJV)

Paul gives us 15 different characteristics that describe true love. And over the years, much has been said and written about each of these. What's most profound is the fact that every believer is already filled with God's love based on Romans 5:5. God's love is available to live in and through us as we are being changed more and more into Christ's likeness. What this means to you is that you are being changed into each of these different characteristics. As you grow in Christ, you should be able to come to a point where you can put your name into this verse. For example, can you say you "suffer long", you are "kind", and you "don't envy"? Go through each characteristic and place your name before it. This is your life goal: to become more and more the likeness of true love. And the promise is that if you become more like the love of God, you too will *"never fail"*.

This is what today's verse means to me.

_____

_____

_____

_____

_____

_____

Here is how I can apply this truth in my life.

_____

_____

_____

_____

_____

_____

This is my prayer for today.

_____

_____

_____

_____

_____

Daily Devotional– Day 32

"Owe no one anything except to love one another." (Romans 13:8 NKJV)

Every believer in Christ has an I.O.U. Yes, we're all in debt and owe everyone. We're not speaking of money, or property, but of the love of God. We are in debt and owe others God's love.

So stop and think about those people in your sphere of life. Consider your parents, siblings, kids, friends, and co-workers. Do you owe them anything? Yes, you owe them love. You're in debt to them in love. You may not owe them financially, but you do have an obligation to give them love. You do have a responsibility to care for them, be kind to them, and show mercy to them.

Some may ask, "What about those around us who have hurt us, abused us, and taken advantage of us? Do I still love them?" Yes! Remember, Jesus even said, "Love your enemies" (Matthew 5:44). Do we put ourselves in unsafe situations? No, but we do in some way or capacity pray for and love even those who hurt us.

So today, think about ways you can show love and kindness to another person. Can you speak well of, honor, and bless those around you? Can you give a compliment, send an encouraging word, and say thank you? Remember, you owe others love; now go give it away as God gave His love to you.

This is what today's verse means to me.

_____

_____

_____

_____

_____

_____

Here is how I can apply this truth in my life.

_____

_____

_____

_____

_____

_____

This is my prayer for today.

_____

_____

_____

_____

Daily Devotional– Day 33

"Above all things have fervent love for one another, for 'love will cover a multitude of sins.'" (1 Peter 4:8 NKJV)

Peter said, *"above all things!"* Apparently what he had to say was vitally important for all to hear. So let's pay attention. He said, *"above all things have fervent love"*. This, my friends, was a top priority for Peter and now is also for us. We're not to have just passive love, or say we have love, but our love is to be fervent. Our love for each other is to be shown, demonstrated, fervent, real, and authentic.

Many believers say they love, but in some circles it's hard to find. However, let your sphere of life be a place where you freely offer love to others in word and actions. Be known as a person of love.

The end result, Peter says, is that "love will cover our sins". One of the strongest motivations for loving is the opportunity to share in God's love, covering and forgiving sin. Too many people make mistakes and bear the shame of them. But our love for each other covers, hides, and diminishes sin, and highlights God's mercy and compassion. So today, go offer someone true love and help *cover up* the wrongs around us. AMEN!

This is what today's verse means to me.

_____

_____

_____

_____

_____

_____

Here is how I can apply this truth in my life.

_____

_____

_____

_____

_____

This is my prayer for today.

_____

_____

_____

_____

_____

Daily Devotional– Day 34

"And I have declared to them Your name, and will declare it, that the love with which You loved Me may be in them, and I in them."
(John 17:26 NKJV)

When you think about God, or hear someone talk about Jesus, what first comes to your mind? Is it a God who condemns, judges, and is ready to hold your life in the balance between heaven and hell if you make a mistake? Or when you think and hear about God do you sense and feel His love, compassion, and goodness?

Jesus shared who the Father was with His children. He did so with the anticipation that they would know and experience the Father's love too. Jesus declared who the Father was with the intention of His hearers growing in and becoming more at rest in His Father's love. So the more they heard, the more they knew of God's love.

This truth teaches us that the more you know about the Father, the more you'll know about His love. He reveals more of Himself so that we know more of His love. So, today, if you want to experience His love, get to know the Father more. Ask Jesus to reveal more of the Father, and thus you'll know more of His love. You'll soon discover that He's been close to you all along waiting and longing to love you deeply and have you know and rest in His love.

This is what today's verse means to me.

_____

_____

_____

_____

_____

_____

Here is how I can apply this truth in my life.

_____

_____

_____

_____

_____

_____

This is my prayer for today.

_____

_____

_____

_____

Daily Devotional– Day 35

"God so loved that He gave. . ." (John 3:16 NKJV)

Love gives. Love doesn't take. Love blesses, encourages, lifts up, honors, supports, provides, approves, and cheers on. Love fills the longing heart, heals the broken, shines on the downcast, quiets the fears, and absolves the failures. Love gives.

God, being love, gives as an overflow of who He is. As the new song says, "He didn't want Heaven without us". He wanted to share who He was with us for eternity. In fact, we're told that in the ages to come we're going to experience the exceeding greatness of His grace toward us (Eph. 2:7). There will be a continual unfolding of His love for eternity.

We will never fully comprehend the greatness and extent of His love in the giving of His son. This is incomprehensible to our finite minds. God gave the closest and best of Himself in exchange for you because of His love for you too. But this is who He is, a giver. In giving His Son, we see there are no other limits to His giving to you. What else do you need in life? What desires, hopes, and dreams live in you waiting to be fulfilled? God is so interested and passionate about His love for you that He gave it all so that you too can come to know Him and experience Him. Today, thank God for giving to you. Thank Him for His gift, His Son.

This is what today's verse means to me.

_____

_____

_____

_____

_____

_____

Here is how I can apply this truth in my life.

_____

_____

_____

_____

_____

This is my prayer for today.

_____

_____

_____

_____

What did God do in my life this week?

What is my testimony of God's work this past week? What did the Holy Spirit say to me? What prayers were answered? Who did you share Christ with? What good thing can you thank God for? Write out the difference this week made in your life.

_____

_____

_____

_____

_____

_____

_____

_____

_____

_____

_____

_____

_____

Week Six
The Hope of Heaven

VIDEO NOTES

_____

_____

_____

_____

_____

_____

_____

WARM UP

1. What do you think Heaven will be like?

2. Do you have any idea what we'll be doing for eternity in Heaven?

3. Is there a favorite activity or hobby you'd like to take with you to Heaven? How about your favorite music of food?

| WORD | "Those who love their life in this world will lose it. Those who care nothing for their life in this world will keep it for eternity." (John 12:25 NLT)

Week Six Big Idea:

The glorious hope of heaven is available to those who believe and receive Jesus Christ.

Within seconds after we die, most of us will be utterly surprised. Things will not be as many of us have believed. We have been taught...

- You don't have to be afraid of dying if you've been "basically a good person."
- You don't need to be spiritual, have faith, or live for God; just avoid really bad things like murder.
- There is no Judgment Day where we'll stand before God to give an account of our lives, no heaven to gain, and no hell to avoid.

Jesus taught none of these ideas. In fact, He made the subjects of life after death, heaven, and even hell as plain as day. In this study, we will consider both the words of Jesus and the testimony of reason in order to discover the hope of heaven.

1. Are there good reasons for believing in life after death?

What happens after we die? While the reality of life after death cannot be proven beyond all doubt, the following indicators can make a strong case that life as we know it is not all there is.

✓ **Science suggests that life after death may be real.**

Medical studies and experiences can also be convincing. For example, in 2014 the largest medical research study ever conducted on cardiac arrest patients was made public. After four years of research, the study concluded that 40% of those studied experienced some form of awareness during the time that they had been declared dead; 46% experienced mental recollections, some including being able to see themselves and describe in specific details exactly what their doctors were doing. *"The findings of the study as a whole suggested that the recalled experience surrounding death now merits further genuine investigation without prejudice."* (Sam Parnia et al., "AWARE—Awareness During Resuscitation, A Prospective Study," Resuscitation 85(12): 1799-1805).

✓ **Humanities suggest that life after death is real.**

Humanities can be described as the body of knowledge that documents the human experience. We use philosophy, literature, religion, art, music, history, and language to understand and record our world, and all of these endeavors have to one degree or another advanced a universal human belief in life after death.

Psychologists know that people of virtually every culture throughout human history have believed *there has to be something more to life than this world. Ethicists* often argue that in light of the existence of both good and evil, it stands to reason that evil must be punished, good must be rewarded, and an afterlife is an essential component in the concept of justice.

Philosophers like Immanuel Kant took the reasoning of ethics and concluded, *If there is a good God and there is morality, there has to be an afterlife for any of life to make sense.* The overwhelming testimony of history and humanities points to confidence in an afterlife.

✓ **Scripture clearly teaches that life after death is real.**

"We die only once, and then we are judged. So Christ died only once to take away the sins of many people." (Hebrews 9:27-28 CEV)

The Bible tells us that there is not only life after death, but that it is an eternal life so glorious that "no eye has seen, no ear has heard, and no mind has imagined what God has prepared for those who love him" (1 Corinthians 2:9). The clear gospel message is that Jesus Christ came to the earth to take on the punishment for our sins and give us the gift of eternal life.

Have you ever read about or seen someone who shared that they died and saw Heaven? What was their experience?

_____

_____

_____

2. What is heaven?

"In my Father's house are many rooms. If it were not so, would I have told you that I go to prepare a place for you? And if I go and prepare a place for you, I will come again and will take you to myself, that where I am you may be also." (John 14:2-3 ESV)

Heaven is a real place described throughout the Bible. The word "heaven" is found 276 times in the New Testament alone. After Christ's resurrection, "He was taken up into heaven and sat at the right hand of God" (See Mark 16:19 and Acts 7:55-56) where He awaits a great reunion with all of His followers.

Heaven is a wonderful place of "no mores." There will be *no more tears, no more pain,* and *no more sorrow* (Revelation 21:4). There will be *no more separation*, because death will be conquered (Revelation 20:6). The best thing about heaven is the presence of our Lord and Savior Jesus Christ. We will be face to face forever with the One who loved us and sacrificed Himself for us.

Paul encourages us to cling to the hope of heaven and not lose heart. Although we "groan and sigh" in our earthly life, we have the hope of heaven in our hearts (2 Corinthians 5:1-4).

The Bible also speaks clearly of the reality of hell.   For example, Jesus taught about those who did not do the will of God in this life, saying,

> *"These people will go away into eternal punishment, but those with God's approval will go into eternal life." (Matthew 25:46 GWT)*

In fact, Jesus spent more time warning people about the dangers of hell than He did in comforting them with the hope of heaven. This makes the preaching of the Good News of Jesus Christ a top priority for the church.

Why is it vital that we share Christ with our family, friends, and co-workers?

---

3. How can we enter heaven?

God has provided the keys to open the doors of heaven in Jesus, who said "I am the way, the truth, and the life..." (John 14:6). All who believe in Christ and receive the forgiveness of sins by faith in Him will be granted entrance into heaven. For those who reject Christ, heaven is not possible. Jesus said, "Whoever believes in the Son has eternal life, but whoever rejects the Son will not see life, for God's wrath remains on him" (John 3:36).

The entirety of the Christian life is a celebration of the resurrection and a preparation for the return of Jesus Christ and a glorious future in heaven. As Paul encouraged us,

> *"Since you became alive again, so to speak, when Christ arose from the dead, now set your sights on the rich treasures and joys of heaven where he sits beside God in the place of honor and power. Let heaven fill your thoughts; don't spend your time worrying about things down here. You should have as little desire for this world as a dead person does. Your real life is in heaven with Christ and God. And when Christ who is our real life comes back again, you will shine with him and share in all his glories."* (Colossians 3:1-4 TLB)

Why is believing in Jesus Christ central to entering into Heaven for eternity?

_____

_____

_____

_____

Conclusion:

Do you have reasons to hope for an eternity in heaven? Life after death is real. Heaven and hell are real. And forgiveness and eternal life are real. Have you made a decision to receive Jesus Christ as Savior? If so, you have the hope of heaven in your heart. If not, we invite you to pray today:

Dear God, I know that I am a sinner and there is nothing that I can do to save myself. I confess my complete helplessness to forgive my own sin or to work my way to heaven. At this moment I trust Christ alone as the One who bore my sin when He died on the cross. I am grateful that He has promised to save me despite my many sins and failures. Father, I thank you that I can face death now that you are my Savior. In Jesus' Name, Amen.

APPLICATION

1. Have each group share briefly about the time they discovered the reality and joy of knowing they were going to Heaven.

2. Heaven and hell are real. Now that you know Christ, discuss ways to help others come to know Him and enter Heaven.

PRAYER

1. Pray for anyone who does not know the Lord or anyone with doubts about their salvation.

2. Pray for each group member to have the opportunity to share the truth of Heaven with their friends and family.

Digging Deeper

Bible verses about Heaven

For the interested Bible student, an enlightening study would be to go through the following verses and outline the numerous descriptions, activities, and blessings of Heaven.

For further study have the members of the Life Group each pick a couple of verses to bring to the group meeting and share their insights.

1 Corinthians 2:9	John 14:2	Psalm 33:6
1 John 5:5-8	John 3:1-36	Psalm 73:24
1 Peter 1:4	John 3:13	Revelation 11:19
2 Chronicles 6:30	John 3:16	Revelation 12:7-9
2 Corinthians 5:1	John 5:29	Revelation 14:13
2 Kings 2:11	John 6:47-50	Revelation 2:7
2 Peter 3:10	John 6:50-71	Revelation 21:1
2 Peter 3:13	Lamentations 3:41	Revelation 21:1-27
Acts 7:49	Luke 12:32	Revelation 21:1-4
Colossians 1:12	Luke 12:33	Revelation 21:1-5
Colossians 3:4	Luke 15:10	Revelation 21:18
Ephesians 1:18	Luke 20:34-36	Revelation 21:19
Genesis 1:1	Luke 23:43	Revelation 21:21-25
Hebrews 11:10	Matthew 11:25	Revelation 21:22-27
Hebrews 11:16	Matthew 13:43	Revelation 21:27
Hebrews 12:22-24	Matthew 18:10	Revelation 21:4
Hebrews 13:14	Matthew 19:21	Revelation 22:1-5
Isaiah 45:18	Matthew 25:46	Revelation 22:15
Jeremiah 10:12	Matthew 3:12	Revelation 4:1-11
Job 22:12	Nehemiah 9:6	Revelation 7:9
Job 9:8	Psalm 103:11	Romans 1:18
John 10:28	Psalm 19:1	Romans 5:17
John 13:36	Psalm 20:6	Titus 3:5

Bible verses about Hell

Jesus taught much about the reality of hell. In fact, He spoke three times more about Hell than Heaven.

Below is a list of scriptures about Hell, its eternal nature, pain, and the eternal consequences of denying Christ and living for self.

While it may not be the most popular study for a small group, nevertheless, it is sometimes a needed discussion. Have the members review some of the scriptures and share them with the group.

Degrees Of Punishment In Hell – Rev. 20:12-13
Fire Of Hell – Matthew 13:30
Hell Is Everlasting – Matthew 25:46
As An Experience – 2 Thes. 1:8-10
As Incentive To Action – Matt. 7:13-14
Description Of – Luke 16:23
Punishment Of – Rev. 20:10
Occupants Of Hell – Rev. 19:19-20

Matthew 5:29-30	Revelation 19:20
Matthew 18:9	2 Peter 2:4
Matthew 5:29	Matthew 23:33
Matthew 10:28	Revelation 20:13-15
Matthew 5:22	Matthew 8:12
Matthew 7:13	Revelation 20:14
Matthew 18:8	Matthew 13:47-50
Matthew 25:46	Luke 16:19-31
Matthew 12:32	Revelation 14:9-11
Mark 9:47-48	Luke 16:23
2 Thessalonians 1:8-9	Matthew 25:41

Daily Devotional– Day 36

"But God, who is rich in mercy, because of His great love with which He loved us, ⁵ even when we were dead in trespasses, made us alive together with Christ (by grace you have been saved), ⁶ and raised us up together, and made us sit together in the heavenly places in Christ Jesus." (Ephesians 2:4-6 NKJV)

You are living in two worlds at once. The first is here on earth in the natural realm. The second is seated with Christ in heavenly places. The moment a person is born again, they are raised up with Jesus and seated with Him far above all principalities and powers in the heavenly realm.

It is from that place that you can choose to live your life on earth. This is a place close to the Lord, siting with Him, a place of fellowship and worship. It is a place where you hear from the Father and live in victory over sin and darkness. The key, though, is living the life of Christ with Christ on this earth. This is why you as a Christian are called to live in God's presence near him, while on earth. We can then be His ambassadors of good news now, today, where we live. We can bring heaven to earth. So today, pray for God's presence and anointing everywhere you go and in all that you do.

This is what today's verse means to me.

_____

_____

_____

_____

_____

_____

Here is how I can apply this truth in my life.

_____

_____

_____

_____

_____

_____

This is my prayer for today.

_____

_____

_____

_____

_____

Daily Devotional– Day 37

"Let not your heart be troubled; you believe in God, believe also in Me. In My Father's house are many mansions; if it were not so, I would have told you. I go to prepare a place for you." (John 14:1-2 NKJV)

Just hours before Jesus was crucified, He told His disciples that He was going to go and prepare a place for them. Was Jesus speaking figuratively or literally? Is there an actual mansion for you in Heaven? This is what Jesus said, "In my Father's house are many mansions". We really don't know much more than what we read here. The word mansion in this verse is used only once in the New Testament, and it means a dwelling place, or abode. What's important though is that Jesus states that He is going to prepare a place for you.

You do have a place of dwelling, rest, and joy in God's presence. There is a place of abiding with God by His Spirit where He quiets your soul and fills you with His joy. This is why He said to not let your heart be troubled. So today, don't be troubled about the events and ungodly circumstances filling the world. Know this: Jesus has prepared a place and that place is with Him, where the enemy can't go and where His peace fills all. So thank Him today for this place that He prepared, and let Him quiet your soul.

This is what today's verse means to me.

_____

_____

_____

Here is how I can apply this truth in my life.

This is my prayer for today.

Daily Devotional– Day 38

"If I go and prepare a place for you, I will come again and receive you to Myself; that where I am, there you may be also." (John 14:3 NKJV)

Jesus Christ desires to be with you. He promised to never leave you. He promised never to forsake you. (Heb. 13:5). Jesus told His disciples at the last supper that He was going to prepare a place and then come back for them so they could be where He was.

Jesus then died and rose again. A place is now prepared for you. And Jesus poured out His Spirit so that you can be filled with Him, His power, His presence, and His grace.

Notice the wording in the verse above, *receive you to Myself.* Believers in Christ need to know they are welcome to come into His presence, and He'll receive them. The Bible says you can come boldly before Him (Heb. 4:16). You can come and dwell in His presence any time you desire, and He'll welcome you. It is a beautiful experience that as we live and carry out our life on earth, we also sense His presence in all we do. This is Christ's desire, for His presence to fill you, heal you, and guide you at all times. So today, know that Christ receives you and desires you to fellowship with Him. Take the time to worship Him, bless Him, and thank Him for this tremendous opportunity and blessing.

This is what today's verse means to me.

_____

_____

_____

_____

_____

Here is how I can apply this truth in my life.

_____

_____

_____

_____

_____

_____

This is my prayer for today.

_____

_____

_____

_____

_____

_____

Daily Devotional– Day 39

"He will wipe away every tear from their eyes, and death shall be no more, neither shall there be mourning, nor crying, nor pain anymore, for the former things have passed away." (Revelation 21:14 NKJV)

There is a time coming when all tears, death, mourning, and pain will be wiped away. There is a place off in the future where there is pure joy, peace, rest, healing, and fulfillment.

But what about today? While the future promise of Heaven is exciting, what about all the pain and tears today? The answer is in Jesus' prayer where He said for us to pray, "Your Kingdom come, your will be done on earth". This prayer shows that we can believe for a manifestation of what Heaven is like on earth. The Bible says that He can turn our mourning into joy (Psalm 30:11). We're told that He can give us the oil of joy for the spirit of heaviness (Isaiah 61:3). Further, we read weeping may endure for the night, but joy is coming (Psalm 30:5).

So today, thank God that one day every tear will be wiped away, but know that your tears can be wiped away today. Yes, you don't have to wait for the future, you can pray for Heaven's joy to come your way today. Believe it, pray for it, and allow the Holy Spirit to minister this grace to you.

This is what today's verse means to me.

_____

_____

_____

_____

_____

_____

Here is how I can apply this truth in my life.

_____

_____

_____

_____

_____

This is my prayer for today.

_____

_____

_____

_____

_____

Daily Devotional– Day 40

"But our citizenship is in heaven, and from it we await a Savior, the Lord Jesus Christ, who will transform our lowly body to be like his glorious body, by the power that enables him even to subject all things to himself." (Philippians 3:20-21 NKJV)

There has been a lot of news these days regarding U.S. citizenship and people from other countries being here illegally. This discussion has become very political. For some it is a painful experience. For many there are numerous opinions, angry positions, etc. . . .

The Bible shows that regardless of what your citizenship status is, a person who is born again has become a citizen of the Kingdom of God. This mean you can actually have dual citizenship: one in the U.S. and one in the Kingdom of Heaven.

As a citizen of the Kingdom of Heaven you have all the rights, privileges, and opportunities that come from living in God's kingdom. You have His provision, protection, possibility, and potential. You live in freedom from the enemy as Jesus Christ is King over this Kingdom.

Today, thank God for the opportunity and blessing of living in His Kingdom. And today, live as a citizen from Heaven. Lift up your head, stand tall yet humble, and live with confidence in God's Kingdom.

This is what today's verse means to me.

_____

_____

_____

_____

_____

_____

Here is how I can apply this truth in my life.

_____

_____

_____

_____

_____

This is my prayer for today.

_____

_____

_____

_____

_____

Daily Devotional– Day 41

"The Father loves the Son, and has given all things into His hand. ³⁶ He who believes in the Son has everlasting life; and he who does not believe the Son shall not see life, but the wrath of God abides on him." (John 3:35-36 NKJV)

Notice the phrase, *"he who believes in the Son has everlasting life"*. Everlasting life is not something you get off in the future. It is something you have now. Yes, there will be a transition someday in the future. But the point is you don't have to wait to begin living the blessing of everlasting life and can actually start receiving it today.

Eternal life is not so much a time element as it is a quality of life component. Eternal life is the ZOE life of God. It is that life which is above the mundane affairs of this life. God's life, eternal, is not controlled by the events of this life. God's life is a power, an ability, and supernatural life which lives above, in dominion, and with authority over darkness, defeat, and despair.

Today, choose to live God's eternal life. It begins when you repent of sin and confess Jesus Christ as your Lord and Savior. Once that's done, the Holy Spirit begins to work in you the eternal life, the nature of God and power to overcome all things. So thank God today and begin living life – eternal life – the God kind of life – eternal life.

This is what today's verse means to me.

_____

_____

_____

_____

_____

_____

Here is how I can apply this truth in my life.

_____

_____

_____

_____

_____

This is my prayer for today.

_____

_____

_____

_____

_____

Daily Devotional– Day 42

"Beloved, now we are children of God; and it has not yet been revealed what we shall be, but we know that when He is revealed, we shall be like Him, for we shall see Him as He is." (1 John 3:2 NKJV)

When Jesus is revealed to this earth as the risen Lord and King, we shall be like Him. Friends, a transformation is going to take place in the future. We will put off our old body and put on a new body. We'll put away sin, defeat, and death and put on the robe of righteousness and stand with Jesus Christ. It is at that point that we shall be like Him.

But before that day comes, the Holy Spirit is at work in each of us, conforming us into the image of Christ. You don't have to wait for that day. You can start living like Him today. Sure, when we see Christ, we'll experience His fullness. But there are levels and degrees of Him that we can start experiencing now.

It is God's Holy Spirit that can work in you to cause you to be like Him. It is God's presence and power that daily works in you to reflect the character and power of Jesus Christ.

Off into the future "we shall be like Him". But even so you can choose to be like Him now. It takes a decision and a prayer to step into God's likeness. Believe it and walk in it – AMEN!

This is what today's verse means to me.

_____

_____

_____

Here is how I can apply this truth in my life.

This is my prayer for today.

What did God do in my life this week?

What is my testimony of God's work this past week? What did the Holy Spirit say to me? What prayers were answered? Who did you share Christ with? What good thing can I thank God for? Write out the difference this week made in your life.

Notes:

Made in the USA
San Bernardino, CA
21 March 2018